Being A First Church

What A Pastor's First Congregation Should Know

By

Mark E. Yurs

Wipf and Stock Publishers
Eugene, Oregon 97401

Being A First Church:
What A Pastor's First Congregation Should Know
By Mark Yurs
Copyright 2003 by Mark Yurs

ISBN: 1-59244-165-3

Wipf and Stock Publishers
199 West 8th Avenue, Suite 3
Eugene, Oregon 97401

To

St. John's United Church of Christ
Belvidere, Illinois

With Gratitude for
Nine Happy and Formative Years
1982-1991

Contents

Contents

Foreword

A minister's first church after ordination is a long-awaited field. Imagined, dreamed about and feared, it is a novice minister's first real opportunity to test gifts for ministry and the call to ministry. This book is about that church and what it can do with and for its new pastor.

A good experience in one's first church is like a first love. It is never forgotten and never replaced. Other churches may be served and loved later on in one's career, but the quality first church occupies a special place in pastoral affection. Even though long years go by, the one who served it once still rises up to call it blessed.

A negative experience in one's first church can have one of two results. At best, a bad experience can make a person wiser the next time around. A good bad experience, as it were, can make a pastor tougher, stronger, less apt to be taken advantage of in a later situation. At worst, a bad experience early on can drive a good pastor out of ministry. The person who has had a bad experience and has quit serving in pastoral ministry can be left doubting his or her abilities and call or, worse, despising not only this church but all Christian congregations.

This book is written to help first churches realize their unique opportunities and help them to provide positive experiences. It is written in the hope that the more positive experiences there are, the longer pastorates will become and the happier they will be. It is written in the further hope that longer and happier pastorates will lead to stronger and happier churches, enabling them to be communities of greater faithfulness and effectiveness. In short, it is written in the hope that quality first experiences will redound to the glory of God, both in the hearts of individuals pastors and in the lives of individual congregations.

I write as one who can claim the truth of Psalm 16.6a: "The lines have fallen for me in pleasant places..." (RSV). That is to say, I write as one whose experiences in ministry by and large have been happy. The paths of God's leading took me along a route that went straight from high school into college and immediately thereafter into seminary. I graduated from seminary in May of 1982 and was ordained in June. I had been called by my first church two months before I graduated, but did not begin there until the first of June. I did not leave until nine years later, when I came to my present church where I have been for twelve years. I am grateful to God for the two churches I have been privileged to serve. The first was, and the second is, supportive, understanding, graceful, loving, and more. I know what the psalmist means when he rejoices, "The lines have fallen for me in pleasant places..."

Much of what follows is autobiographical. It is that not because I am interesting or a genius or skillful. Rather it is because I believe I have been treated well by the people God has given me to serve. My stories are really the stories of their gracious actions. They rather than me are the heroes of these stories insofar as there are any heroes. By naming how these churches, particularly the first, have helped this pastor, I hope to indicate how any church can help its pastor develop a better self-understanding as a minister and better relationship to the work of ministry.

The material I proffer is written for the uncomplicated church. As I put those two words together, I realize the phrase is an oxymoron, for every living church is somehow complicated, messy, and full of fits and starts. Only dead churches are finally uncomplicated. Still, I use the term to indicate that I have in mind the church that is free of deep-seated and intractable pathologies that get in the way of serious conversations and sane relationships. A church filled with those kinds of troubles can unravel a veteran minister in short order. They are no place for innocent rookies, and denominational placement officers, insofar as they have opportunity and ability, should keep innocents from landing in them. By indicating that I am writing with the uncomplicated church in mind I am saying that my focus is not on helping the dysfunctional church behave magnanimously, but on helping good churches do their best, particularly when it comes to seizing the unique responsibility and opportunity that come with being a pastor's first church.

There are a number of people who have made this project possible, and I want to use this opportunity to speak a word of thanks. I am grateful to my Association Minister, the Rev. Dr. Robert D. Mutton, for encouraging me in this task, reviewing the initial drafts, and providing opportunities to learn more of what is needed for today's new pastors and to test some of my thoughts. I am likewise grateful to the members of the Ministerial Development Group which meets, under Bob's guidance, biweekly in my office. Though many of them are so much newer to the work than I, they are so much wiser than I ever was or can ever hope to be. Their open-hearted sharing has helped me process my own experience and grow in my understanding of ministry.

Professor Elmer Colyer of the University of Dubuque Theological Seminary has encouraged me along the way as well. His words of support and his practical helpfulness have come at just the right time and have been sustaining.

My thanks go out to the spouses who responded to my request for help with Chapter Six. Their insights and stories were indispensable in helping me think through what ought to be said regarding the spouse of a first time pastor.

I am grateful, indeed, to my wife, Sherrol, and our three children, Lena, Laura, and Dale. Not only have they been generous in not begrudging me computer time, they have been true partners in the now twenty-one years I have served as a pastor. Among the five of us, I am the only one who is ordained, but they each are ministers indeed. I would not have lasted in the work of the parish without them.

A special word of thanks is reserved for St. John's United Church of Christ, Belvidere, Illinois, my first church. Those who were part of that fellowship from 1982 until 1991, and who have a tender place in my heart today, witnessed my first awkward steps as a minister, picked me up when I fell, cheered when I stood, followed where I led, led where I did not know how to go, and showed patience when I was slow to follow. Because they helped me grow up as a minister, this book is lovingly dedicated to them, with deep thanksgiving.

Chapter One

What the New Pastor Needs

In an old movie called *One Foot in Heaven,* Frederic March stars as Will Spence, a man trained in medicine who takes up pastoral ministry instead. When he and his wife arrive in the small town where his first charge is located, no one from the congregation is expecting them. The station-master who drives them by way of a horse-drawn wagon from the depot to the parsonage calls out to passersby, "Meet the new minister!" This, much to the station-master's delight, sends the congregation's parsonage committee scurrying into action, and soon word of the Spences' arrival reaches everyone. One by one, members of the parsonage committee and others of the congregation appear at the house, introduce themselves to the new couple, and try to hide the fact that they are completely caught off guard and unprepared. This was not the beginning anyone had in mind.

My first charge started in ways exactly the opposite. A group of men from the church brought a truck to my hometown and, with a contagious spirit of camaraderie, loaded my meager belongings. When we arrived at the parsonage, we were met by more men of the same spirit. Together they unloaded the truck into a neat house, freshly painted inside and out, and surrounded by beds of flowers in bloom. These people were ready for their new pastor and anxious to help him arrive with comfort and joy.

Moving day does not make or break a ministry, but I am firmly convinced the experiences a pastor has in his or her first parish can do much to determine the future course of his or her ministry. Certainly first charges are not necessarily solely responsible for someone's success or failure, but they can mightily contribute to success or failure. Seminary is able to do much, but it cannot do everything. The difference between being in seminary and actually serving a church can be compared to the difference between reading a romance novel and actually falling in love. The one is theoretical; the other is experiential. Ideas formed in seminary - ideas about one's own self, about ministry in general and churches in particular - meet reality in congregations. This meeting can be friendly or frightening. It can get a newly ordained graduate off to a good start in ministry or bring a fledgling ministerial career to an acrimonious end. Thus, a first church has the opportunity to do what no seminary can possibly do - it can help a new minister who has long thought about ministry actually discover what ministry is like and, hopefully, fall in love with pastoral life and work.

Seizing this opportunity with grace, charm and effectiveness demands something of the church and its people. A congregation that calls a veteran pastor can make certain assumptions the congregation who calls a novice cannot. By the same token, in order for a novice's ministry to get off to a successful start, the congregation that is a first charge has to have a kind of savvy the congregations served later in life do not. Much of this is because the veteran has developed a style, comfort and degree of toughness the rookie has not begun to formulate. Quality first charges love an inexperienced pastor into ministry in ways that allow for the formulation of the style, comfort and toughness later years will require.

We are not talking about going easy on a new pastor. The congregation that is a first charge will neither shield nor excuse its pastor from rigorous work, but it will not expect him or her to be able to take to the work like an old pro. It will not treat the minister with kid gloves but it will put forth a kind heart full of understanding as to the difficulties of beginning a new career in a demanding profession. Let's look at some of the best gifts a church can offer someone fresh from seminary.

Prayer

An Old Testament story can help us picture the singularly important work parishioners perform when they pray for their pastors. Some of you may not appreciate that this story has the backdrop of battle, but if you are willing to see that ministry can be a daily struggle which can tend toward fatigue, you may be less inclined to dismiss this Exodus tale. The details can be found in Exodus 17. This chapter has the Israelites engaged in battle against the Amalekites at Rephidim. Moses is the leader, of course, but Joshua is the commander in the field. Moses watches the battle from a hilltop. Joshua and the Israelites prevail over the Amalekites but only as long as Moses holds his walking stick high in the air. The trouble is, Moses' arms weary. Aaron and Hur, who are with Moses, find a rock he can sit on, but that does not help him keep his staff in the air. His arms begin to sink, and whenever they do, the Amalekites get the upper hand against Joshua. When Moses can no longer hold his heavy arms and heavier walking stick above his head, Aaron and Hur stand on either side of him providing the strength Moses can no longer find in himself. These three upon the hill, together with Joshua and his soldiers down below, win the day. To relate this to the parish, your prayers for your pastor can be as Aaron and Hur were to Moses, and so empower him or her for a work that takes more strength of spirit than a single soul can muster.

Turning to New Testament materials, we can notice the Apostle Paul, who spoke of being engaged in spiritual welfare (Eph. 6.12), requested the prayers of his people (Eph. 6.19; Col. 4.3; 1 Thess. 5.25; 2 Thess. 3.1). If this leading apostle needed the strength which comes from a praying congregation, how much more does the newcomer to ministry! Parishioners sometimes think we pastors have a direct line to God which makes matters of the spirit crystal clear. We do not. The work of ministry is beyond us. We are often beside ourselves when it comes to knowing the will of God in our own lives, much less that of the church or of its people. We pray, to be sure, but our prayers, spoken in the loneliness of our own devotional lives, can feel like they are those of Hamlet's father - our words fly up, but our thoughts remain here below. Like Paul, we who pastor today need the strength that comes from the intercessions of others who pray for us.

More than anything else, the pastor fresh from seminary needs prayer, for this is what makes ministry possible. Ministry is intensely spiritual and it requires spiritual strength. This strength can come only from God. In the final analysis, ministry never depends upon the power of personality, the strength of intellect, the force of will, or the gift of gab. It depends upon God, who is Lord of the church. God is ready to supply every congregation and every servant, both clergy and lay, with all things needful for effectiveness as disciples. To receive what God is ready to give we must be perpetually open to God and in communion with God. This is the realm of prayer, the realm without which no minister can succeed and no pastor can prosper.

The vast majority of parishioners who pray for their pastors will do so during the course of their personal and private devotions. I would like to encourage as many as I can to pray not only *for* their pastor but also *with* their pastor. What I have in mind is this. Your pastor prays with you regularly. Meetings of boards and committees in many churches begin with a prayer said by the pastor. Hospital calls and counseling sessions often end with prayers spoken by the minister. Worship services generally incorporate a pastoral prayer which has the minister gathering up the joys and concerns of the community and lifting them to heaven with supplication and thanksgiving. Often the best and most meaningful of these prayers, at least from our human perspective, are those which name specific persons and particular needs. I have spent over twenty years praying these kinds of prayers and I have come to view them as some of the most important as well as most rewarding work I do. There is a singular joy that comes from holding a person before God in prayer.

Still, what I have craved over those same twenty years is the blessedness of *hearing my name* spoken in prayer. The few times this has occurred have been cherished moments, and I covet even more. While I am aware people in the church do pray for me, I would love to be present when they do. My suggestion is that you offer your pastor this gift from time to time. You may never see what it does for his or her soul but it could be one of the finest contributions you make toward the welfare of your entire congregation.

Time

All pastors need time when they first move into a parish; those who are moving into the ministry need even more. Seasoned veterans need time when they start out in any new charge. One of the rules of thumb we are taught is that we need to spend the first months, perhaps even the first year, surveying the field. Certainly a pastor knows something about a congregation as soon as a call is accepted, but living with a congregation over a period of time teaches so much more about the congregation's life, history, traditions, hopes, and relationships. This "getting to know you" period works both ways, of course, as the congregation gradually becomes accustomed to new person who now occupies their pulpit and pastoral office. Just now, however, let us think about what the minister must learn.

When a pastor arrives at a new church, one of the first orders of business is to learn the names of the new parishioners. This comes more easily for some than it does for others, but those first weeks when few names are known are awkward for all. Parishioners may little understand how difficult it is to preach to a congregation of strangers. Thus, even worship is uncomfortable at first. In time, however, names and faces become familiar and relationships begin to grow.

The minister needs to learn the personality of the parish as well as the names of the parishioners. This is among the chief reasons why it is said that the better part of wisdom is for the pastor not to introduce any changes or initiatives for the first year. It takes that first year of walking with a congregation through the seasons of the church to learn how a particular people lives its life as a community of faith. This opens the way for the minister to learn the cherished traditions of an individual congregation. These traditions touch everything from who puts up the Christmas tree to who stays to clean up after congregational meetings. Along the way, the minister who lives with a community of faith through a cycle of the church year learns much about the way this community lives out its faith. Ideally, as this learning takes place, pastor and parish begin to fall in love with each other, initial nervousness begins to fall away, and a certain level of trust begins to develop. Only then is the pastor in a position to introduce new programs, ideas or initiatives.

The pastor new to ministry as well as to the congregation being served needs to learn all this and more. Thus the congregation that calls a recent seminary graduate needs to be prepared to give their new minister the gift of time. The next chapter will take up the issue of the work of ministry and the idea of a model of ministry, but at this point it is appropriate to mention that a model of ministry is essential. What is a model of ministry? A model of ministry is one's self-understanding of the work ministry requires and of the approach one takes to that work given one's own talents and abilities. Seasoned veterans have a model of ministry; novice pastors need to grow into a model of ministry. Learning the people, history, and traditions of a parish can take up to a year; coming to a model of ministry can take much longer.

A couple of personal examples may prove useful at this point. The first relates to preaching. I am not a lectionary preacher, and many of my colleagues, most of whom are lectionary preachers, rib me and make gentle sport of my maverick ways. I was some four or five years into ministry, however, before I discovered that I am not a lectionary preacher. I did preach the lectionary my first three years in the field. When I branched out in my fourth and fifth years to try something different, I found that I came into my own as a preacher. This is what I mean by needing time to grow into a style or model of ministry.

The other example to bring forward relates to pastoral counseling. There are ministers who have regular appointments with certain parishioners over a period of time and engage with them in a kind of clinical work the main aim of which is therapeutic. My calendar, however, is not full of counseling sessions. I am no therapist. I try to help people, of course, but the help I offer is a form of pastoral guidance and care. I pray with people and try to help them find God and relate to God; I do not delve into their psyche or probe the depths of their subconscious. That is work for others, not me. While I respect psychology, I am no specialist in it or practitioner of it. It took me a long time to express this without guilt, for somewhere in the recesses of my mind I had the perception that clergy spend significant periods of time counseling their parishioners through their problems. Getting rid of this guilt has made me more confident about what I can actually offer my people, and I believe it has made me more effective in what I do.

The point is, ministerial self-perceptions and approaches to the work take time to develop. No seasoned veteran can hit the ground running the moment the interim pastor vacates the premises, and no rookie can begin knowing full well who he or she is as a pastor. The congregation who calls the recently ordained needs to be ready to grant their new pastor this time to marinate into ministry. Only then will their raw reverend begin to become a seasoned pastor.

Freedom to Fail

Success in ministry is difficult to determine. Failure in ministry is easy to spot. Courage for ministry keeps one going when success is hard to find and failure easy to notice. Unless clergy develop this courage, they are not long in ministry. Congregations cannot give their pastors the courage they need, but they can give them the freedom to fail. By the freedom to fail, I mean a willingness to go along with a new idea and the readiness to offer subsequent grace when the new idea does not work quite as well as the minister had planned. If the pastor knows he or she has this freedom to fail, the fork in the road which separates the way of timidity from the way of courage will find him or her taking the way of courage. This way leads to the potential of growth and maturity, for both congregation and pastor; the way of timidity leads, again for both pastor and parish, toward stagnation.

I first experienced the freedom to fail on the very first day of the summer job I had all through college and seminary. It was working as a groundskeeper and maintenance man for our local park district. The park had a mid-size tractor and a two-wheel cart, and my boss asked me to back the wagon into the area where we needed it. I no longer remember how many times I jack-knifed that little rig before I got it into place, but I do remember my boss did not say a word. Perhaps it was because he was being paid by the hour, and if it took me all day to get that thing backed up, he would earn just as much laughing on the inside as he would sweating on the outside. The point is, he let me keep trying until I got it right. By the end of that summer, I was very efficient at backing up our tractor and wagon, and imagined I could do as well with an eighteen-wheeler using only the mirrors. By giving me the freedom to fail - miserably, I might add - my boss gave me the confidence of succeeding.

The first church I served gave me the freedom to fail when, rather early during my time there, I proposed a scheme for training some parishioners to do the work of evangelists. The plan involved the husband of our organist at the time. He was a devout and sincere man of faith experienced in providing training in evangelism for lay people. What complicated matters was that he was from a denomination different from ours and more conservative. He assured me, however, that he would adapt his materials to fit the theology of the United Church of Christ and our congregation's personality. I proposed this plan to our Board of Elders, who approved of it, and I recruited people to become part of the first training session that was to take place. As it turned out, everything was in order but only during the planning stage. Five minutes into the first training session, it became embarrassingly clear to me and to those whom I recruited that nothing had been adapted to fit us. The material was theologically restrictive from our point of view. It did not fit the personality of our congregation, either. The program seemed to call for an "in-your-face" style of highly aggressive evangelistic work. I was embarrassed. I imagined that the lay folks I had recruited would turn on me. I figured I had just lost every chance I had of being successful at recruiting in the future. Grace prevailed instead. My worst fears did not come true. Everybody concerned acknowledged that this plan did not work but no one came to the conclusion that no plan I devised would ever work. This was a lesson in mercy from a kind and generous people, and it left me with the courage to try again even though I had failed at first.

Remember that we said new ministers need time to develop their model or style of ministry. This is going to involve a lot of trial and error. New clergy will begin and perhaps strive to emulate a beloved professor from the seminary or revered minister from the home church. This is natural and to be expected. It is, in part, the way ministers grow. Not a little of this will seem awkward. In time, the new pastor will feel like young David marching forth in King Saul's armor. That is to say, the new minister will soon discover, and the congregation will know, the mentor's style does not fit. Another style will be tried for a time. There may even be a period of role confusion within the minister. With help from God and grace from the congregation, the new pastor will get it right and courage and confidence will grow. This will keep him or her in ministry when success is hard to see and failure is easy to spot.

Encouragement

As the new minister tries and fails as well as attempts and succeeds, one of the best gifts the congregation can offer is encouragement. We can look to Jesus to find the pattern of encouragement to follow. According to facts reported in Luke 10, he appointed seventy persons and sent them out upon a mission of proclaiming the Kingdom of God and of healing. The circumstances to which Jesus sent these seventy were hardly ideal. They were, he said, like lambs being sent straight into a pack of wolves. Not only was there no guarantee of success, there was expressed the distinct possibility of failure.

Luke does not allow us to see these seventy engaged in their mission, but we are present when they return and report to Jesus. Would that we had this exchange on videotape, to see the joy on Jesus' face and hear it in his voice as he enters into the enthusiasm of his friends who are, through the exercise of ministry, discovering the gifts for ministry which they possess through him. They are breathless in their return to him; they are full of joy and excitement as they tell what they were able to do, much to their own surprise. "Lord, in your name even the demons submit to us!" This exclamation elicits from Jesus the response: "I watched Satan fall from heaven like a flash of lightning." Clearly, he, too, is thrilled both by what they were able to do and by what they are learning about themselves as servants of the gospel.

We find in this exchange between Jesus and the seventy two forms of encouragement. Jesus encourages the disciples, first, by entrusting them with important yet difficult work. Being entrusted with an errand of this nature is almost always a source of newfound strength for it opens a person to see there is someone who believes in them and their abilities. Receiving the trust of respected person helps one rise to the occasion with a self-confidence that might not otherwise be available.

Second, Jesus enters into the joy of his friends' successes. Their joyful return following their missionary activities has them exchanging stories about moments of ministry that went well, and, presumably, about ones that did not go well. The sweetness of victory overcomes the agony of defeat. Above all, the seventy seem to exhibit a spirit of surprise over all they found they were able to do.

"Wow!", they cry, "we could cure diseases and even cast out demons!" To which Jesus responds - and I think he is broadly grinning here - "When you did that, I saw Satan fall!" There is much these freshly enthused disciples do not know about ministry and mission, but Jesus saves all that for later. Now is the time to undergird their success, enter their joy, and encourage their spirits.

Praise such as this may not improve performance but it improves the attempt to do well. My wife has noticed this when working with youngsters who are making ready to sing in a Christmas program or other event. By complimenting each one or the group as a whole about something, the confidence level of everyone almost immediately grows. When it comes to that particular part of the song in the next rehearsal or at the actual performance, all belt out those notes with pride and joy. And Satan falls.

Satan will fall when you give your pastor positive comments about what you think he or she does well. All this will help establish your pastor's sense of self and of ministry. It will work to build high ideals, for, if told by you that this is done well, your pastor will not want to disappoint you the next time around and will strive to do even better.

Constructive Criticism

Since your new pastor is still learning there will be imperfections close to the surface of ministry and within rather plain view of the entire congregation. Unfortunately, what is in the plain view of the congregation may be missed by the fledgling minister. This brings us to think about constructive criticism, which is also something every new pastor needs. I hesitate to broach this subject, for I fear giving sanction to petty complaining under the guise of constructive criticism. More than a few congregations are full of people who seem to think *their* criticism *is* constructive. The reality is that nearly everyone knows how to complain but the one who can be genuinely helpful in complaint is comparatively rare.

Where critical remarks are concerned, we are at a point of particular vulnerability for the pastor fresh from seminary. The rest of us in the ministerial office have developed something of a crust but the rookie has yet to be toughened by experience. What is more, previous experience outside ministry, even and especially seminary experience, cannot quite prepare new clergy for what happens in the parish with regard to wagging tongues. Some of the reason for this lack of preparedness is rooted in the difference between seminary days and parish life. One thing that happens as the pastor moves from seminary studies to parish ministry is that evaluation, offered regularly, clearly and openly by a veteran teacher on the subject at hand, is exchanged for criticism issued at uncontrolled intervals from any number of persons within the church and about any subject which may come to mind. Sadly, this criticism often makes the rounds of the parish before it reaches the pastor. Thus, at a time when the inexperienced minister could most benefit from serious and informed feedback, there is nothing but uncensored talk.

Constructive criticism of ministerial practice is directed to the minister instead of scattered about the town. It differs from common complaint in that it is offered at an appropriate time, sticks to one subject at a time, and suggests a possible solution every time. Let's look at a simple case that could have been disastrous for my present ministry had not a woman from the church befriended me with constructive criticism in the early days of this pastorate. I had received, from the interim pastor, and double-checked its completeness with the church secretary, a list of the congregation's shut-ins. I started making these rounds, with some degree of frequency, before my ministry in this place was very old. I was faithful to the people on the list, and I was feeling good about myself. Then one Sunday one of our Sunday School teachers asked to speak with me in my study. There she told me her husband's grandmother, also a member of the church - elderly but not shut-in - was a bit grumpy because I visited the others confined in her apartment building but not her. The teacher was reporting this information both for my sake and for that of her grandmother-in-law. Her remarks to me were not in a spirit of complaint; she understood that it was too early in my days in this church to know about her husband's grandmother much less to have had time to pay her a visit. This story has a happy ending, for I began including this very delightful woman in my regular round of calling and found myself looking forward to visits with her.

This Sunday School teacher is to be congratulated, for, had she not handled this issue the way she did, my work could have been undermined quite early. Significant numbers of clergy get reputations in their communities as being ministers who never call on the shut-ins when, in fact, they *do* call upon the shut-ins but, for some reason, miss a *particular person* at a *particular time.* No doubt there had been a conversation in the family during which Grandma said the new minister had not been to see her when he was in the building to see her friend down the hall. The family could have spread it around the church and community that the new minister plays favorites, ignores the elderly, doesn't call enough, or some other such thing. Had that gotten around, a hole would have been dug for me and I would have had a hard time getting out. But the granddaughter-in-law came to me privately, shared what was on her relative's mind, and suggested I give her a call. A pastorate was saved through constructive criticism!

Allies

As the above remarks concerning constructive criticism make clear, no pastorate, young or old, can survive without allies. Allies are people who stand with the pastor in helpful ways. The Apostle Paul had scores of people around him, as indicated by those passages which appear late in nearly every letter, by which he sends greetings to his fellow workers. Still, he reports a situation in which no one stood by him except the Lord (2 Tim. 4.16-17). As a pastor and as a person, Paul relied upon the Lord very much, but the company of another Christian at such a time as this would have been a boon to his soul. This, however, is not the time to speculate as to Paul's situation or the state of his soul; rather it is occasion to see that no pastor today need stand alone, especially not one who is new to the work.

Some of the most helpful allies are those who are eyes and ears in the congregation and community. These are not gossip mongers, but caring friends who know the family connections that exist throughout the congregation and the news of the community. They help the pastor know when someone is hospitalized, facing surgery, grieving the loss of a distant relative, or worried about some other matter that burdens hearts. Without wishing to promote stereotypes, allies of this nature who prove the most helpful to me are elderly women. Their circumstances are such that they can no longer contribute to the work of the church in the ways they did in previous years, but the help they provide me, especially in knowing about hospitalizations and day surgeries, is immeasurable. They are ministers indeed who help ministry happen. When they call, they often apologize for telling me something I may already know; but I reply it is better to hear something repeated than to have people assume I know when in fact I do not. Their help to me is priceless. Without this team of women, I would hardly be able to pastor. They help me know what I need to know.

It should be said, of course, that no one, whether young or old, male or female, who assumes this role in the congregation, should suppose they are compiling the minister's "to do" list. The caller may know who is in the hospital but this knowledge does not extend to what is already on the minister's agenda for the day or week. The caller should not expect their ringing of the parsonage phone to send the minister sliding down some kind of fireman's pole and into action. Every pastor has to do a certain kind of triage every day to determine where his or her activities are best spent at that particular time. After he or she hangs up the phone from talking to some ally about some congregational need, it may be most appropriate for the minister to do nothing more than pick up reading where he or she was when the phone rang.

Allies of another kind are those who help with conflict or potential conflict. Here the image may come from basketball. As a team sport, those who handle the ball most require help from their teammates who may seldom hold the ball. These others set picks. Simply put, they stand like poles to block opponents while the ball handlers safely dribble around them and score points. The score book does not record anything about the player who set the pick, but without his work the more acclaimed star would be less effective and the team would lose.

Churches and pastors need persons who set picks. These are allies to the minister in that they realize not every concern needs to rise to the level of criticism or complaint. By way of a listening ear, let us say, they can hear somebody spout off about something and then promptly forget about it. Thus they have helped a parishioner vent while they have shielded the whole church from standing in the wind. These kinds of allies have a depth of knowledge and a gift of discernment. Their knowledge extends to the persons and personalities of the parishioners, and they further know how to discern whether an issue raised is critical or petty. They allow pettiness to die for lack of a second, and they follow through in appropriate ways regarding that which is critical.

Up to this point we have been thinking about what the new pastor needs. As you have been reading, perhaps you have been thinking of persons in your congregation who could supply this or that need much as they have in the past with reference to former pastors. It remains to be said, however, by way of a cautionary note, that there occurs a reconfiguration of relationships in churches when pastors change. Those who were close and effective allies to the previous pastor may not be able to do as well in this role with reference to the new pastor. It could be they will not be able to serve in this fashion at all. To say this is not to pass judgment or cast aspersions; it is only to recognize human nature. Some folks are able to "hit it off" with certain people, but not others. Maybe an excellent way to help the new pastor is to show Christian kindness to those who were close to the former pastor. The more they are able to mourn their loss in a healthy way, the more spiritual and emotional energy they will have to begin a good relationship with the new pastor.

Chapter Two

What Your Pastor Does

You have recently called a new pastor, and you are anxious to have him or her settle into the work of the church. You can be of significant help to your new pastor if you and others of your congregation come to an understanding of the nature of pastoral ministry. But what is the work that ministers do?

Pastoral ministry is a profession few lay persons understand. To say this is not to slam the laity. It is simply a facing of facts. All of us are lay persons with regard to someone else's occupation and not many of us understand the work other people do. Ministry falls into line with this. Folks who are part of the church see ministers on a regular basis, but most persons outside the clergy have but a scant inkling of what it is pastors do.

I recall a time from my youth when I met our pastor in the local post office one weekday morning. School, which was not in session at the time, was all I knew. It was the only way I knew how to structure my time. I could not conceive how anyone not in school could pass the time of day! Without speaking to my minister about this, I wondered how he could find enough to do all week long.

My wife grew up in the Baptist tradition. She and her family were active in their congregation, and they became quite close to the pastor and his family. Not only did these families spend significant time together inside the church, they socialized together outside the church as well. Even given all this, Sherrol reports she did not realize everything that goes into being a minister until she married one and started living in a parsonage.

A parishioner who lovingly nurtured me with good humor in my first church, enjoyed joking that I only worked an hour a week. She laughed about feeling sorry for me during Lent when midweek services were added and I had to work two hours.

What does a minister do all week long?

One of the peculiarities of today is that the church itself is struggling to find an answer to this seemingly simple and straightforward question. Seminaries, denominational hierarchies, local congregations, and individual pastors are trying to determine just what ministry is. Ministry probably was never as easy to describe as we suppose it was when we take nostalgic looks to the past, but those glances backward in time show there appears to have been then more widespread consensus and less confusion among all concerned. Andrew W. Blackwood, a foremost teacher of ministers during the 1930s, 40s, and 50s, and himself a parish pastor for 17 years prior to 1930, loved to speak about the ideal minister spending morning hours in the study, afternoon hours among the people, and a crowning hour in the pulpit.

Whether or not such a pastor ever existed, Blackwood's description came before society started changing in the ways it has over the last forty years, taking the church along with it. Even a casual glance at the lifestyles of most people today will show the impossibility of Blackwood's ideal having much of a chance now. Morning hours in the study? Maybe in the office, but we are hard-pressed to use all the hours for study, as Blackwood suggested. The church office is a busy place these days; as more people have fewer hours they can volunteer, much of the machinery for running the church is left to the minister. Afternoon hours among the people? Maybe nursing home visits and hospital calls, but hardly anybody is home in the afternoon any more. Besides, if the minister *did* drop in the person who answers the door may drop dead. Old-fashioned pastoral calling is just that; it seems to be out of date. A crowning hour in the pulpit? Before we can get there, we have to spend evening hours back at the church in a seemingly endless cycle of meetings.

None of this says anything about the ways the image of the pastor has changed over the course of the same forty years. There was an earlier day when the minister's place in church and community was not questioned. The minister was a person of respect, education, authority, and even power. Now there are others in the community and perhaps even the church who have more respect, education, authority and power than the pastor. Clearly, today is not yesterday. That would be all right if only we could be sure what day this is. Church and society are in a transitional time, with the lives and lifestyles of people changing to new economies, new systems of communication, new encounters with the world, and more.

Where does the pastor fit in? What does the pastor do?

The answer to this question is called a "model of ministry." Simply put, a model of ministry is an understanding of the work of ministry in light one's understanding of the nature and purpose of the church as informed by scripture and tradition. It is a statement, or at least a framework, of self-understanding that guides one's perceptions of and approach to the various tasks of the pastoral office. It is a sense of the specific work a person believes Christ has called him or her to do. Without a model of ministry in view, it is difficult to maintain the integrity of the pastoral office and sanity in the minister's mind. If there is no model of ministry, if one just follows the "in-box" way of doing ministry - which is to say, one simply does whatever a parishioner asks whenever they ask it - the pastoral office becomes a kind of brothel where people are free to request any service they desire and the minister is not free to refuse.

Early on in a pastorate, whether the pastor in question is a recent seminary graduate or a member of the clergy long ordained, it is not unusual for conflict to develop over models of ministry. The pastor, on the one hand, formulates expectations of the congregation and goes about the business of the day according to one model of ministry. On the other hand, the congregation as a whole, and individual members of it, begin to line up their expectations of the pastor and for themselves as Christians in terms of other models. These differences of opinion over what constitutes authentic ministry and congregational life may not erupt into a full-blown controversy in the church, but they can be slowly simmering behind every board meeting, in every relationship, and around every issue.

The principle adopted here is that ministry is enhanced when pastor and people unite under a model of ministry that is meaningful to both. Hopefully, the church has sifted through some of this during the search process as the congregation or its designees developed the congregational profile that was circulated among candidates for the vacant pastorate. Ideally, the search committee gave attention to this as candidates emerged and were interviewed. Nevertheless, no matter how candid these conversations around ministry and congregational life were, as the work of ministry begins and as pastoral relationships begin to take shape, both with individuals of the church and with congregational structures, ideals and expectations once again become the topic of necessary conversations. Now that pastor and parish are known commodities to one another, as it were, the model of ministry under which they unite needs to be revised or at least revisited.

The more recent an inductee into the ranks of the clergy a minister is the less settled he or she is into a particular model of ministry. A good seminary helps its students articulate a model, and the best seminaries help students devise one that is true to the realities of congregational life. Yet no seminary is able to give any student a "one-size-fits-all" model of ministry that would suitably clothe every pastor, much less every parish. Thus your newly installed pastor will be doing some tailoring. Language learned at the seminary, and used in the interviews with the search committee, will be let out, taken in, hemmed, and re-stitched as the new minister tries it out in the parish. Given time, a good minister will come into his or her own. A good first church will grant this time.

It should be pointed out that no model of ministry worthy of the name will accept the status quo of the congregation wholesale. There may be much about your congregation that is worthy of acceptance, but ministers work to change congregations. This is because we are all followers of Jesus, and Jesus always calls us to further discipleship and development. Whenever Christ says, "Follow me, " he does not stand still. He moves on ahead. So must the church that bears Christ's name. For this reason, quality first churches will expect their pastor to have a model of ministry that will challenge them rather than pacify them.

There are any number of models of ministry on the market. As with most things on the market, not all are of high quality. Some see the church in the same light as a secular business, and expect the pastor to be something like a chief executive officer. Some view the church as a kind of corporation in which the members are the stockholders and the pastor is the lone employee. Others, often folks outside the fellowship, consider the church to be something like a secular social service agency and think of the minister as the coordinator of volunteer relief efforts. Persons in the church, and often within the denominational hierarchies, look upon the parish as a moral voice in a community and hope the preacher will exert energy as a social prophet or community activist. More common among the people is a model of ministry that loves the local church as the caretaker of the soul, curator of religious rites, and guardian of various rites of passage. Such a view of the church understands the minister to be a chaplain who does little more than say the appropriate prayer at the appropriate time. Also common among the people is a model which sees the church primarily as a place of worship where they expect the minister to be liturgist and preacher.

My own perspective is that each one of these carries some modicum of truth but no one of them is an adequate representative of the whole truth. Were we to settle on any one of them, we would be settling for a diminished view of the church as a whole, including its people as well as its ordained leadership. Equally false and harmful would be a lumping of all of them together as though the pastor is all things all the time. Such a grab bag "ministry is whatever we need at the moment" is less a model of ministry than of ministerial fatigue and breakdown. Who can fill that kind of role? Who, in all good conscience, can expect anyone to fulfill that role?

For the remainder of this chapter, I would like to articulate a model of ministry that makes sense to me. I believe this model squares with biblical faith and Christian tradition, especially the Reformed tradition in which I do my work and which is, I suspect, the tradition of the vast majority of my readers. I believe this model is also fit for these times which seem so uprooted and full of change for the church. This is not the only model that might be apropos today, but it covers the territory an effective and faithful model should encompass. Local church conversation around this model can be a starting point for developing a suitable model for your particular community.

What the Church Is

Ministry is rooted in the church, so every legitimate model of ministry begins with a consideration of the nature and purpose of the church. The description which follows is not contingent upon church size. While the tiny country church and the suburban mega-church may be as different as night and day, they have in common all that follows.

The church is *a community of the called.* "You did not choose me," said Jesus, "but I chose you" (Jn 15.16). While these words were spoken to the disciples in the Upper Room on Maundy Thursday, they apply to all Christians. That is to say, we are in the church because Christ has called us. We are not part of the church through our own doing. We are not in the church by way of family legacy, birthright or inheritance. We are not in the church because we have shopped around and found Christianity to our liking and this congregation suitable to our tastes. We are in the church because Christ has called us. This is why we use the word *ecclesiastical*, and its relatives, when we refer to matters church-related. This English word is rooted in a Greek word which means *to call out* as when people are called out for an assembly. The church is ecclesiastical, called out, called into being. It is not self-generated. It is a community of persons who have responded to the invitation extended to them by the grace of God.

The church is *a community of praise.* There is a New Testament scene, told in the Gospel According to John as well as Matthew and Mark, in which a woman opens a classy looking jar and pours very expensive ointment over Jesus. Those who are watching, including the disciples, think this is a ludicrous act because of its wastefulness. They take a business-like approach and determine that this woman's actions are not cost-effective. Who would pay all that money just to dump the whole jar all at once? Jesus, however, receives the act with grace and tones down those who are counting costs. Acts of praise, as in the case of this anointing, are not best measured with dollar signs. This little episode teaches us, among other lessons, that worship is the main thing for Christians, the primary duty against which all others are to be measured. According to the Westminster Confession, which Presbyterians especially seem to appreciate, the purpose of human beings is to glorify and enjoy God forever. This same purpose exists for the church. The community of the called answers with praise. Worship is the chief function of the church.

This opens us to see some of the inaccuracies of those models of ministry which look upon the church as something like a business. The church is nothing like a business. Businesses have a profit motive; churches have a worship motive. Businesses have a customer to please; churches have God to praise. Businesses see issues through the lenses of their budgets; churches view their budgets through the lens of worship. Both the church and the business are interested in fiscal responsibility, but for different reasons. The business is interested in fiscal responsibility for the sake of solvency, whereas the church trusts solvency and is fiscally responsible for the sake of the glory of God. Consequently, where a business defines fiscal responsibility in terms of cutting expenses, the church speaks of fiscal responsibility in terms of stewardship, and understands that it is in giving that we receive. From a business perspective, the woman with the ointment did the wrong thing, a foolish thing. From a doxological perspective, which is the perspective of the praise of God, this "foolishness" was the better part of wisdom.

The church is *a community of the text.* Scripture plays a foremost role in the life of the church because the Bible shapes our understanding of ourselves and our world. It does so by telling the stories of our spiritual ancestors, particularly as those ancestors perceived God calling them to life and into relationship with God and with one another. These stories give us our language for speaking about God and God's activity today. Our main purpose for scripture study is not to learn what God did yesterday, but to discern, in light of what God did yesterday, what God might be doing today and calling us to do and be tomorrow. Thus the themes of scripture are ours and we look back upon the Bible in order to look out upon today and interpret our own lives as being lived under God.

The church is *a community of proclamation.* "So faith," the Apostle Paul wrote, "comes from what is heard, and what is heard comes from the word of Christ" (Rom. 10.17). This makes sense in a community that sees itself first of all as a community of the called who respond with praise. We are a people rooted in the word. More appropriately, we are a people rooted in the capital *W* Word, for Jesus is the Word of God made human flesh. This Word of God still addresses us, and, in addressing us, calls us to life and relationship.

The Reformed branch of Christianity has long given proclamation of the Word priority. We honor but two sacraments, Baptism and Holy Communion, but proclamation has in our view a sacramental quality. That is to say, we believe that, much like Christ is present through the sacraments, the Holy Spirit can and does touch our common human words in such a way that they become the Divine Word or a vehicle for God's presence among the people. The Apostle Paul indicated something of this when he wrote to the Thessalonians, "We also constantly give thanks to God for this, that when you received the word of God that you heard from us, you accepted it not as a human word but as what it really is, God's word, which is also at work in you believers" (1 Thess. 2.13).

The church is *a community of service.* The church is a doing community as well as a listening community. Those who are true to the gospel they hear live as servants of the Lord whom they trust. Those who are true to the gospel they hear understand, along with James, that "faith without works is dead" (Jas. 2.26) and that they are to be doers of the word rather than merely hearers of it (Jas.1.22). Likewise, they understand Jesus' parable of the two builders which teaches that the proper response to the word is to put it into action (Mt. 7.24-27).

To call the church a servant community is to indicate that it exists for others. Emil Brunner, a Swiss theologian of the middle and late twentieth century, is well known for saying, "The church exists by mission as fire exists by burning." We are in the church for a purpose and not for a privilege. The purpose we have is to give of ourselves. According to the United Church of Christ Statement of Faith, God "calls us into the church, to accept the cost and joy of discipleship" and to be God's "servants in the service of others."

It is important to recognize that every Christian has some such servant role. Service is not limited to the person in the pastoral office. One of the contemporary distortions of the church looks upon it in much the same way society looks upon a store, seeing it as a place where goods and services are provided by the minister, who is seen as something of a shopkeeper. A faithful view of the church sees it as a community of believers all of whom are engaged in mission for the sake of Jesus Christ. While pastors are set apart for a leadership role, all Christians are called by God and made priests and servants in the mission of the gospel.

Who the Minister Is

Having considered what the church is, we are now in a position to begin delineating who the minister is and what the minister does in this context. I believe it is best to identify the minister as *a servant of the Word*. This places the pastor directly under the authority of Jesus, the Word of God, who calls the Christian community into being and who reigns as the Lord of the church. It likewise prevents us from ever properly thinking of the pastor as a mere employee of the church who works for the congregation serving the whims of its members, boards and committees. It opens us to see, more appropriately, that the minister is one who works in a congregation and hopes to serve the will of God for that church and its people.

The Word whom the minister serves is Jesus. Since Jesus is the Risen Christ, he is our living Lord still actively at work in the power of the Holy Spirit to guide and shape congregations as well as individual Christians. As indicated earlier, this living Lord who addresses persons today and still asks them to follow along in active discipleship does not stand still. Thus the servant of the Word will of necessity be one who hopes to lead the congregation to further development as opposed to one who labors to maintain the status quo at all costs. Good ministers are unavoidably agents of change - not for change's sake, but - for the sake of Christ and the spiritual nurture of the congregation.

Thus far we have been using the term *minister* to refer only to the person who is ordained. In truth, by virtue of baptism, all Christians are ministers, servants who exercise some gift or gifts of the Holy Spirit for the good of all (1 Cor. 12.7). Some congregations even have their bulletins read:

FIRST CHURCH

Ministers:	All the Members of the Congregation
Pastor:	Rev. Smith

This is a printed method of giving voice to the Protestant principle known as "the priesthood of all believers." This doctrine means that all Christians have a certain right to teach, preach, witness, hold positions of authority in the church, pray with and for persons, and so forth.

Where does this leave the pastor or ordained minister? He or she is one who is set apart for special authority in the church as pastor and teacher. As a servant of the servants of God, the ordained minister is set apart from - not above - the other members of the church to occupy the preaching office, administer the sacraments, and exercise spiritual oversight. This leads us to say more about the tasks of pastoral ministry.

The minister is a servant of the Word who *serves the Word through prayer*. The single most important thing a pastor does is pray. *The Evangelical Catechism*, which was used extensively in the Evangelical Synod of North America, one of the precursor denominations of the United Church of Christ, defines prayer as "conversation of the heart with God for the purpose of praising [God], asking [God] to supply the needs of ourselves and others, and thanking [God] for whatever [God] gives us." However prayer is defined, it is absolutely essential to ministry. Christ is the Head of the church, and prayer is the chief means of being in contact with Christ's leadership. Christ is the Lord of our lives, and prayer is the chief means of being in fellowship with this one who is supreme.

By way of prayer for the church, the minister seeks the spiritual guidance that is necessary for leading the church in the direction God intends. By way of prayer, the pastor holds the members of the church, individually and as a whole, before the one who is the Shepherd of souls and who alone has the answers people need. By way of prayer, the pastor seeks to maintain what is her or her best relationship; and, by way of prayer, the pastor seeks to help others develop a similar relationship with God.

Nothing can be accomplished without prayer. A prayerless church is an ineffective church; it may be a busy organization, but it is not an obedient or effective faith community. In the previous chapter we noted that the disciples could do what Jesus did. They could even cast out demons. But not without prayer! There was an episode where a possessed person was brought to the disciples, but no matter how hard they tried, they could not rid the young man of the demon inside him. After Jesus successfully performed the exorcism, the disciples, to their credit, asked why they had been unable. Jesus replied, "This kind can come out only through prayer" (Mk. 9.29). Along these same lines, a church without prayer is a church that is in a weakened state.

Not only is prayer vital to congregational life, it is absolute essential to pastoral life. If a pastor does not draw from the deep well of prayer and all that comes from the devotional life, he or she will soon become spiritually depleted. This depletion will manifest itself in terms of physical exhaustion, emotional strain, and a wide variety of other maladies not easily traceable to the spiritual life but certainly rooted there. Ministry simply cannot take place without prayer. Prayer is not your pastor's favorite hobby or even professional specialty; it is the key to your pastor's life.

The minister is a servant of the Word who *serves the Word through study*. After carrying the umpteenth box of books from my house to the u-haul truck, one of the men who helped move me to my first church quipped to my mother, "I hope he doesn't spend his time reading these books because we've got things for him to do!" It was a joke, and everyone knew it. (I would come to know this man as one who values study and learning - he purchased his first computer well after his 90th birthday and learned how to use it so his mind would not atrophy!) He knew the value of reading, but I tucked his quip away as a reminder that not all parishioners would think the same about time spent in study.

Since the church is a community of the text and since the pastor is set apart to be the preacher and teacher who interprets the text to the community, and so the community to itself, study is as indispensable to ministry as prayer. When the Pilgrims were about ready to set sail for the New World, their pastor, John Robinson, who stayed behind to minister to the part of the congregation that did not cross the Atlantic, preached a sermon in which he declared, "The Lord has yet more light and truth to break forth from His holy Word." Hopes such as this make study of the Bible an integral part of a pastor's regular routine of work. As we read and study the Bible, in a spirit of prayer and with the best helps scholarship can offer, we hope to encounter - not a preachable text we can take to the pulpit next Sunday, but - the living God who is Lord of the church. We are ever at Bible study because God, in the power of the Spirit, uses the Bible to address Christians today, lead the church, and advance the cause of the gospel.

The Bible cannot be studied properly in isolation from other books and resources. Through books of theology, church history, Christian and secular biography, sociology, psychology, and even mystery and other fiction, the student of the Bible can gain insight into scripture and the Lord made known through the text. Since all of life is God's, no subject is wide of the mark when it comes to learning about God and God's ways in the world among human beings.

In a television interview, Sandra Day O'Connor, Associate Justice of the United States Supreme Court, described her average work day. She described a day that is full of reading, followed by more reading, and then capped off with some reading. The wider demands of the parish keep a pastor from reading this much, but, like Justice O'Connor, pastors need to spend significant and concentrated amounts of time reading. Prayer strengthens our souls; reading expands our minds; reading in a spirit of prayer deepens our spirits, and prepares us for service in the church.

We do not read simply for the sake of preaching but we certainly do read for the sake of preaching. We read because preaching demands it, and the minister is a servant of the Word who *serves the Word through preaching*. As a community of the called and a community of proclamation, the church depends upon preaching. The sermon matters. Congregations know this. Church members may grumble about sermons that are long or boring or both, but, whenever they search for a new pastor, they pray for one who can preach. All this is because Christians believe God still uses preaching to save sinners and guide saints.

When it comes to wondering what a minister does, it should be apparent that much of the week is spent making ready for the pulpit. The task of preparing sermons is always on the pastor's mind. Sundays roll around with relentless regularity, and we need to have something to say each week. A friend of mine used to keep a toy cement truck on his desk as a reminder to himself and others that a preacher is always turning something over in head or heart for Sunday, just as the cement mixer is always churning on its way to its destination.

This is not the place to speak about all that goes into sermon preparation, but many parishioners are curious as to how long it takes their pastor to make ready for the pulpit. One dusty sentence in the attic of old preaching textbooks calls for one hour of preparation for every minute of delivery! There may be a sermon or two that calls for that; others can be developed much more rapidly. None should be slapped together quickly. Most ministers will, I think, say that it is difficult to tell how long it takes to prepare a sermon. The actual writing of it may take, say, four hours; but it may have taken a lifetime to come up with the thoughts behind what is written during those four hours. Certainly it may have taken another four hours and more to read what the Bible says, contemplate what others have said, discover what ought to be said today, and discern how it should be said on Sunday.

The point to be kept in mind here is that no church ever wisely begrudges or seeks to limit the amount of time its pastor spends making ready for the pulpit, for preaching is chief among the responsibilities a minister has. God still comes to us through the proclamation of the Word.

Closely related to the work of preaching is the work of teaching. The minister is a servant of the Word who *serves the Word through teaching*. In the typical parish, the minister teaches Confirmation classes, Bible studies, new member classes, and Adult Sunday School classes. Teaching of this nature is essential if the spiritual lives of our people are not to be stunted. Sermons can be filled with teaching, but the pulpit cannot accomplish enough by itself. People are helped and the congregation is served when members of the congregation grapple with scripture in conversation with others, when they dig deep into the themes of Christian theology and learn the basic vocabulary of the Christian faith. If people know the language of the faith, their ability to participate in and draw help from worship is enhanced, as is their ability to pray, to witness to others, and understand their own lives in light of divine truth.

To think of the minister as the pastor and teacher of a congregation is not to limit the teaching that takes place in the congregation to the minister. As a matter of fact, the minister may not be the most gifted teacher among the membership! Others can and should teach. Nevertheless, except in the rarest of circumstances, the minister is the one person in the congregation who has received the most substantial theological training, and this gives him or her both a special opportunity and special responsibility to teach. Ordination to ministry and the call to a particular parish convey a certain authority upon the pastor as the one designated to teach and safeguard Christian tradition as well as biblical interpretation.

The leadership of public worship also occupies a substantial portion of a minister's time and thought, for the minister is a servant of the Word who *serves the Word through worship*. We have already noted that public worship is the primary activity of the church; the ordained minister is the one designated to oversee the church's life of worship, including the administration of the sacraments.

To be sure, there are others who join the minister in the work of planning for worship, such as the organist and choir director, should a congregation be blessed enough to have those leaders, but the pastor has the determinative role. This extends to the selection of hymns for congregational singing, selecting or writing the prayers for unison recitation, determining the portions of scripture to be read, preparing calls to worship, words of assurance, benedictions, and making ready to offer whatever extemporaneous prayers or remarks may be required. In short, the preparation of Sunday's liturgy can be as time-consuming as the preparation of Sunday's sermon.

Some of us do this work in blocks rather than all at once. For example, I plan my sermon topics for an entire season of the church year at the same time, usually just before the previous season closes. Once I settle upon my themes for that season, I select the hymns for congregational singing. I then give that list of topics and hymns to the organist and music director so they can plan their work accordingly. The anthems, offertories, preludes and postludes they select do not have to match my selection of themes exactly, but, as a staff, we seem to think worship is enhanced when there is some correlation between many, if not every one, of the movements of worship. Generally on Monday morning, I compose the other worship materials that will be used the very next Sunday, put them in their proper order, and hand them to the church secretary so she can plan her work for the week, too, and be able to run off the bulletin without being in a rush herself. On Thursday the secretary has me proofread the bulletin and make any last minute changes that may be required. The duplicating and folding of the worship bulletin is done by the secretary on Friday. When worshipers take one of the folders from a greeter on Sunday morning, they may not realize the number of people who have had input into it or the number of hours that have gone into preparing it, but, if we have done our work well, it will be a useful tool to guide them in the worship of God.

In addition to all these public acts, the minister serves privately among the people as servant of the Word *through pastoral care*. This is the work of visitation, hospital calling, counseling and other personal conference. In the best churches, the minister is not the only one who provides this kind of care giving; but in every church the minister is the one who brings a special presence when he or she acts in this way. The minister carries into the home, hospital room or other setting the pastoral office of the church and, in this sense, is something of a sacramental presence whose presence is a reminder of the loving care of the God who never leaves us. Other visitors may bring friendship, warmth, words of prayer and words of faith; the minister alone brings the weight of the whole church. The minister's presence is a reminder that the lonely individual in need is a remembered and valued part of the community.

As with other acts of ministry, the number of hours spent per week performing these functions of Christian love are difficult to total. Some weeks there are more than others, especially if there is a funeral or a number of hospitalized parishioners. Because needs vary from week to week, and because other activities are postponed when pastoral needs are quite intense during a particular week, it is next to impossible and a bit unreasonable, it seems to me, to set a quota for the week. Pressing a pastor to make a certain number of calls in a certain period of time does not respect the minister's ability to discern what is the responsible thing to be doing during any given week or at any given moment. It is certain, though, that clergy will always feel behind in this work and therefore sensitive when criticized about the amount of time they devote to it. There is always someone we can be visiting and with whom we can be praying; there is always someone in need of a word of encouragement or counsel; there is always someone who could benefit from a pastoral call, whether in person or by way of the telephone. This is a never completed task and the amount that we leave undone is unavoidable and haunting.

We ministers are never away from sermons needing to be written, worship services needing to be planned, books needing to be read, classes needing to be taught, visits needing to be made or meetings needing to be attended. Mentioning this last activity helps us recognize the minister is a servant of the Word who *serves through parish administration*. Parishioners may serve on a church committee that meets once a month; the pastor is ex-officio on every board and committee in the church and, hopefully, serves as a member of some committee for the wider church, whether in one's denomination or in the ecumenical community. Needless to say, this fills many evening hours with meetings and many daytime hours with preparations for them.

Within the local church, the minister's administrative role is a fitting part of one's vocation as the congregation's pastor and teacher. Meetings can be splendid opportunities giving the minister occasion to teach about Christian doctrine and duty as the church defines, develops and begins to execute its mission during meetings. They are opportunities to love people into action and help them come to better understandings of themselves and others. Along the way, the minister comes to know his or her parishioners better by working with them in these small group settings.

This survey of what a pastor does is sufficient to show that every minister has more than enough to fill all the days of a week. We still have not said it all, for we have yet to mention clergy are persons with private lives in need of personal time. Those remarks will come in a later chapter. My hope for now is that this much of a model of ministry will begin to help you understand all your pastor is required to be and to do, and so assist you in being supportive of your pastor when others who know less prattle on as if they know more.

Chapter Three

What the Old Seminarian Feels

You may not be prepared to think of your beloved parish as a strange place with unfamiliar practices, but that is exactly what it is to the ex-seminarian who is now your newly ordained minister. Life has been changing rapidly for the person in your pulpit. For the first few months of ministry at least, he or she will be going through something that can only be described as culture shock. Culture shock is a kind of anxiety or uneasiness that develops when one is in wholly new surroundings and without the traditions and conventions one has relied upon in the past. It occurs primarily among travelers, of course, but anyone who loses the anchor of the familiar is susceptible to it. This includes seminarians as they move into parishes.

Coping with culture shock is a key aspect of the pastor's inner life as ministry begins. It is not a problem to be fixed so much as it is an array of emotions to be weathered through. It involves grief over the loss of much that was known and anxiety over exposure to much that is as yet unknown. The best thing parishioners can do is be aware of these emotions and respond with grace, patience and understanding.

Loss of Old Friendships

Graduation days are bittersweet. They celebrate accomplishments and sever ties. They mark achievement and initiate a kind of bereavement. The friendships that made seminary more than schooling are overturned on graduation day, never to be the same again. Pastors fresh into ministry are eager to meet the people of the parish and come to know them with pastoral affection. At the same time, they are missing the friends they made at their alma mater.

Seminary is a time for making new friends. Friendships made during these years have the potential of being quite deep because nearly everyone who begins seminary is at a tender place in their lives. This may be less true for those who came to seminary fresh from college after going to college fresh from high school. It is particularly true for those who have left a career to enter seminary. These folks are in especially new territory. They are, somewhat suddenly, out on a limb financially, emotionally, and otherwise. For the first time in years, perhaps, they are among people whom they do not know. Family life, once structured around the parents' work and the children's schooling, is now structured around at least one parent's schooling, too. What may have been a two-income household is now down to one, while the expense of seminary has sent the family budget sky-rocketing. People in this situation need the support of others, and they find it in other families of the seminary community, all of whom are going through the very same things. All this is the stuff of deep friendships.

Second-career persons are not the only ones to develop close ties with classmates. Everyone in the student body is facing the same struggles semester by semester. Those who have courses in common bear the same burdens at the same time in the form of examinations, papers, and the rigors of academic reading. Students eat together, live together, shop together, watch television together, study together, and talk well into the night together. They support one another and become as close as family, if not closer.

The move into the church upon graduation necessitates a move away from these friends. Certainly new friendships will develop and some of these old ones may last, but, in the meantime, new friendships are not in place and the intimacy that made the old ones rich is now broken. The nearby support of a trusted comrade is gone. It is now impossible to go across the hall and find there one who is working on the same problem, facing the same issue, struggling with the same assignment. Consequently, early on in ministry, a new loneliness sets in upon the parsonage family as a whole as well as upon the pastor him- or herself.

Through no fault of its own, the church community eventually and unavoidably complicates the loneliness that is the loss of old friendships. First churches are often in small towns. Neither church nor town may have many people close to the pastor's age. If the town is in some remote district, even the simple recreation of going to a movie or restaurant may entail more than a little travel. The newcomer is not accustomed to this and needs a period of adjustment.

Now, to be sure, congregations at their best are wonderful communities of believers and the opportunities for fellowship they offer are warmly sincere. But no congregation, large or small, can provide the friends a pastor needs. Pastors and parishioners can and should be friendly toward one another, even closely related, but they cannot be friends in the true sense of that term. Three factors prevent it. One is the charge of favoritism. Perhaps every minister is thought to have "pets" even if the accusation of playing favorites is not overt. Candidly, every minister does have persons in the congregation with whom he or she has a more natural and easy-going affinity. This is human nature and the expectation that it will not occur is unreasonable. Nevertheless, no minister can afford to cultivate the charge of favoritism.

The second factor is more significant. If a friendship does develop between a pastor and a parishioner, the course of life may take them to a point at which the pastoral role is compromised. The issue could be simple disagreement at a committee meeting, conflict between this parishioner and another, or some more personal issue involving the parishioner in a moral, spiritual or psychological dilemma. Experienced ministers treat these matters with sincere pastoral affection, but this is an emotion at least a step removed from that of friendship. This is not to say pastoral affection is less involved or more detached and aloof. It is profound and heartfelt, but also as objective as possible. If a minister loses objectivity through friendship, he or she is not in a place to truly help a parishioner see all that needs to be seen when some complication is staring that parishioner straight in the face.

Thirdly, a minister cannot unburden his or her soul to a member of the congregation as to a friend. Ministry is like war in this regard: loose lips sink ships. A minister cannot talk candidly about one parishioner with another if the subject puts that parishioner in a bad light. To do so would be to sow the seeds of discord and that can reap only damage to congregations, pastorates, and even individuals. Similarly, a pastor cannot speak openly with a parishioner about his or her own life plans because there is some news not healthy for the congregation to hear. To ask a parishioner to keep something confidential is to burden them with a responsibility they may, albeit unintentionally, fail to keep. Were the congregation to learn, say, that the pastor is thinking about looking for another parish, it may lead to feelings of bitterness on the part of the congregation, resentment, and a pulling back from participation. This makes the minister little more than a lame duck and it devastates the friend who spilled the beans.

Loss of Old Routines

New ministers contend with the loss of old routines while they grieve the loss of old friendships. The structured life of the seminary stands in stark contrast to the less predictable pace of the parish. In the seminary, students attend class, complete assignments, receive a grade, have a sense of accomplishment, and proceed to the next course. The tasks associated with these activities are all plainly known up front, the expectations involved are clearly defined, and the evaluation that follows is reasoned, timely, subject-related, open, helpful, and from the expected source. Seminary years are governed by a well-regulated schedule; senior level studies are not required of junior level students, and first semester students are not held accountable for second semester work. All things have their time and there are few surprises.

The parish is widely - even wildly - different. The former student now has a new role. In seminary, one could choose to participate in class or not, and one could select the elective classes that struck one's interests. The pastor is in a leadership position. He or she must stand in the front of the sanctuary and no longer has the option of sitting at the back of the class. This new role carries new responsibility. Whereas the student is responsible for his or her own work, the pastor bears some responsibility for the conditions that exist in the entire church. A student can narrowly focus on one or two subjects at a time; a pastor has to attend to many all at once. The student can know some issues will not come up until the second semester of the second year; the pastor has to face questions that can come up at any time regardless of their inconvenience.

The old seminarian is also in the position of having to prepare a new kind of work product. Seminary work required, in the main, the reading of books and the writing of academic papers. The chief thrust of these papers was to speak to the mind rather than the heart, to the scholarly community rather than the Christian laity. Their main function was to demonstrate how much the student knew; there was no expectation that they help anybody with anything. They were academic exercises. Materials of this nature, important as they are in their rightful place, are rather out of place in the parish. Ideally, the new pastor still submits to the rigors of academic study, but the chief output emanating from one's labors cannot be merely academic. Sermons, prayers, visits, and the like, all of which speak to mind as well as heart, are now the main order of the day. Before it really dawns on the person in the pulpit that he or she is working in a different field, the people in the pews are likely to hear sermons that sound more like essays than messages.

Having said this, I want to hasten to add that I hope you do not expect your pastor to "dumb down" from seminary to parish. You have every right to expect sermons you can understand but that does not exonerate you from the responsibility learning more about the faith you claim. You are still under the call to love the Lord your God with all your mind. This call pertains to those who have never seen a seminary every bit as much as it does to those who have graduated from one. It is incumbent upon every Christian to know the vocabulary of our faith and doctrine. As a colleague of mine used to say to his Confirmands, "There is no percentage in being a clod." If our language for talking about God and our lives under God does not rise above a rudimentary Sunday School level, how can we truly benefit from our faith when we are up against adult concerns? Little sermons and little words lead to little Christianity. Just because your pastor should not talk like a textbook does not mean the pulpit should be as uncomplicated as a coloring book.

Before we leave the theme of the loss of old routines it should be added that the new pastor faces a new constituency. This may be saying what has already been said, but it seems worthwhile to explore it briefly from this angle as well. Under the scheme that was in place before graduation and ordination, the student worked, class by class, for one professor. It did not matter what other professors thought about one's work; all that mattered was what this one professor believed. And this professor based his or her evaluation of the student on an assignment by assignment basis. That is to say, the student was graded according to work specifically assigned, not wider themes not in the purview of the particular course in which the student was then enrolled.

Parish ministry brings a new dimension. Instead of a constituency of one there is a congregation of many. Material the minister prepares needs to take these many into consideration. The task now is to feed the flock rather than satisfy the demands of a single professor. This new constituency is a new culture to which the former student must adapt if the present ministry is going to succeed.

Loss of Chief Mentors

Related to the loss of the old professorial constituency is the loss of chief mentors. One of the joys of seminary life is sitting at the feet of some master teachers who are scholars in their respective fields. One of the regrets from seminary which many graduates have is their failure to really make the most of this opportunity while it lasted. Some of us came to a belated appreciation of a professor, an appreciation we wish we had developed far sooner so more classes could have been taken and more conversations initiated. Those professors whom we did appreciate were relied upon heavily for their wisdom and expertise. We could go to them with questions, profit from their experience, and be guided through complicated issues.

The ex-seminarian is, for the most part, on his or her own. Colleagues in ministry may be near, but, especially early on in a pastorate, relationships with these colleagues have yet to develop. They may be liked, but they are still not known. They are not trusted at the same level a beloved professor was. This leaves the former student feeling alone with problems when they arise. This loneliness can, in turn, contribute to anxiety. It is like being lost in a whole new culture with no guides around.

At this point I would encourage you to believe this is reason enough to do what you can to see to it that your congregation is actively involved in the affairs of the wider church. This will help your pastor make connections and develop bonds with neighboring clergy. My first week at the first church I served happened to fall when our Illinois Conference was having its Annual Meeting. To be honest, my preference was to stay home. I was more eager to begin work in my new church than I was to take off for a long meeting elsewhere. But this church was actively engaged in our Association and the life of the Conference. One parishioner was especially immersed in this dimension of the church. She and I went to the Conference meeting as delegates from our congregation, and she introduced me to many of the persons whom she knew. During one of the breaks between sessions, she introduced me to Merle, the pastor of a neighboring congregation and less than ten years away from retirement. I'll never forget how Merle leaned forward in his chair before our conversation ended and said, "Mark, I want to be your friend." He proved true to his word and was a blessing to me as I started my ministry. This may never have happened if the church I served had been one that kept to itself.

Loss of Old Thought-Patterns

Another aspect of the culture shock involved in the move from seminary to parish is the loss of old thought-patterns. We ministers are trained in a certain way of thinking at the seminary and are left to assume this is the way of thinking that prevails in the parish. It is present in the parish, but it is not the only one that prevails. This leads to a confusion that may get us into trouble out in the field.

The change of thought-patterns is part and parcel of the new constituency we face and the new milieu in which we work. The seminary is an academic community. There scholarship is the standard of authority. One's opinions take on weight and merit when they are in agreement with scholars of note, stated with clarity, articulate and reasonable. The method by which opinions are expressed, supported, assessed, and responded to is fully literary. Communication is in writing. Footnotes matter. Bibliographies count.

Some of this carries over into the parish but not much. Congregational thought-patterns are less interested in major theologians than in the powerful matriarchs and patriarchs of the church. Aunt Mildred and Uncle Artemus mean more than John Calvin and Karl Barth. What the strongholds of this church think is, locally, a more important factor that what the Fathers of the Church thought. The congregation is likely to be less literary than oral. It will appreciate a conversation far more than a written document.

When these thought-patterns clash, progress is stopped. The ex-seminarian can come to a Council meeting with an excellent written proposal regarding, say, the way the congregation will serve Communion. This proposal can be well-thought out, documented with footnotes, backed by the brightest minds in theology today, and brilliant in its treatment of some of the historical discussions that have occurred in the past 500 years of Christian life. But this is the way the seminary does its thinking, not the congregation. To be sure, the congregation does not ignore good theology, but it puts a premium on practical procedures and relational matters. Chances are, the Council will set the proposal aside and make its decision about Communion some other way. It could be they will reach the same conclusion as their new minister but it will be by a different route. As they do, the pastor in culture shock will wonder what happened.

Loss of Anonymity

Pastors are public persons. Their role in the church puts them up front in the sanctuary and out in the open in the community. The smaller the town the larger this truth. Pastors are local celebrities, at least from the standpoint that strangers know their names and faces. We are recognized by people we do not know.

All this is markedly different from seminary life. There we could sit in the back of the class, take an obscure place in the seminary community, and blend into the crowd of the city in which the seminary was located. I attended seminary in Dubuque, Iowa. While Dubuque is certainly no metropolis, it is a big enough town for one to go unrecognized in mall, restaurant, theater, etc. It was extremely rare for me, once outside the seminary building and off its grounds, to run into someone I knew.

I started ministry in Belvidere, Illinois, a town then of 20,000 persons. The vast majority of those 20,000 could go unrecognized wherever they went, even to the nearby shopping mall in Rockford. I on the other hand, had lost the anonymity I had in Dubuque. My picture had been in the paper soon after my ministry started. Shortly thereafter, funerals, civic functions, and other events not limited to my parish brought me wider exposure. It was not long before people I did not know recognized me.

This brings a new scrutiny. Clergy tend to speak of it as living in a fish bowl. It might not be quite that bad, but it is real. The fact of the matter is that we are noticed unbeknownst to us. Those who do the noticing pass judgment upon our ministry and the church we serve. Certainly we do not have to contend with the gaggle of photographers that are constantly around genuine celebrities, but we are not quite in control of when we are out of the public eye. This scrutiny makes us the subject of conversation, and suddenly the quality of our ministry is assessed according to standards such as the way we dress, the age and make of car we drive, the car's cleanliness, the content of our grocery cart, the number of weeds in our garden, and who knows what else.

The realization of this new scrutiny can bring a tremendous amount of stress to one not accustomed to it. If not attended to, it can lead to timidity, loss of confidence, and even deceptive and duplicitous behavior, to say nothing of severe panic or paranoia. Contending with this newfound notoriety is high on the emotional and spiritual agenda of persons new to the ranks of the clergy.

Loss of Traditions

The culture shock felt by new pastors also stems from the loss of familiar traditions. Think alone of the Christmas holiday. Prior to taking up ministry, the pastor celebrated Christmas in a way that was deeply rooted in certain family traditions. Being with family members or special friends is a hallmark of these traditions, as is spending time in certain places and taking part in various festivities and services.

The simple fact is that we who now pastor cannot celebrate Christmas the way we did when we were members of the laity. We cannot go "over the river and through the woods to Grandmother's house" anymore; we have to stay and work. Christmas remains a joyous season, to be sure, but the joy is complicated by a busyness that intensifies up to and through the holiday.

As I have aged in ministry, I have come to appreciate the Christmas Eve services but I have yet to come to them with a spirit of joyful relaxation. As a young pastor, I found them positively stressful. The first Christmas of my ministry was especially so. I wanted to get it right. The church I served had traditions close to those of my home church. There were others I did not know. I needed to learn them so that I did not foul them up, and I needed to succeed with the others so I did not mess them up. Heavy upon my heart was the fear that I would miss something that would somehow take away from someone's enjoyment of their Christmas traditions. Rightly or wrongly, I felt solely responsible for the quality of the congregation's celebration of the holiday.

When we add to this stress of the first ministerial Christmases the fact that we are, perhaps for the first time, away from our own longstanding family traditions, we are close to describing an emptiness. Portions of this emptiness never go away but are repeatedly felt every holiday, chiefly but not exclusively Christmas. Feeling this emptiness for the first time has new clergy conducting their first Christmas services with an inner agony they do not know how to name to their parishioners, and fear they dare not if they could.

Chapter Four

What the Congregation May Never Know

Beginning as early as biblical days, servants of God found themselves to be susceptible to periods of despondency they could not control on their own. Chief among the Old Testament examples is the prophet Elijah. He enjoyed a tremendous success atop Mt. Carmel when he scored a victory over the prophets of Baal. The scene was a contest pitting Elijah and his God against the prophets of Baal and theirs. The story is told in 1 Kings 18 and it is full of action, but none of it from Baal. Both Elijah and the prophets of Baal readied altars and sacrifices to their respective deities, but it was decided they would let the recipient of the sacrifice start the fire. The prophets of Baal strove, under heckling from Elijah, to get Baal to ignite a flame but there was not so much as a spark. The Lord, on the other hand, the living God, triggered such a fire that it even burned up the water Elijah had poured around the altar just to make it more of a challenge. Then, as if defeat were not good enough for them, Elijah had the prophets of Baal killed. We are led to believe this victory so strengthened Elijah that he was able to run ahead of King Ahab's chariot for some seventeen miles!

His thrill of victory is short lived. Ahab and especially his queen, Jezebel, launch a counter-attack aimed directly at Elijah. They put out a contract on him and seek his life. Elijah heads into the wilderness in 1 Kings 19, sits down under a broom tree exhausted, and wishes he were dead. The prophet so full of the joy of victory becomes suddenly overpowered by depression and suicidal thoughts.

The despondency so readily apparent in Elijah is perceptible in other Old Testament characters as well. Among those in whom it can be seen are the psalmist of the 42nd psalm whose poem begins,

> As a deer longs for flowing streams,
>   so my soul longs for you, O God.
> My soul thirsts for God,
>   for the living God.
> When shall I come and behold
>   the face of God?
> My tears have been my food
>   day and night,
> while people say to me continually,

"Where is your God?"
He asks himself repeatedly, "Why are you cast down, O my soul,/and why are you disquieted within me?" He even speaks of being forgotten by God and of walking about mournfully because of the torment inflicted upon him by others.

We can find traces of despondency in the 23rd psalmist as well. That well-known poem speaks of God restoring the soul, so we can presume the soul behind the poem knows something about being downcast and in need of rejuvenation.

More vivid is the picture of Job on his ash-heap, cursing the day of his birth and wishing he had been stillborn (cf. Job 3). His words are certainly those of a despondent man:

> Truly the thing that I fear comes upon me,
>   and what I dread befalls me.
> I am not at ease, nor am I quiet;
>   I have no rest; but trouble comes.

New Testament instances of despondent souls are also readily found. Judas, when he realizes what he has done and the full import of it, commits suicide (Mt. 27.3-5; cf. Acts 1.18-19). Peter, standing on Caiaphas's patio, hears the crowing of a rooster and instantaneously feels the sting of guilt for having denied Jesus; he runs off somewhere and weeps bitterly (Mt. 26.75).

We can likewise detect feelings of despondency in the apostle Paul. Early in 2 Corinthians he speaks as though these feelings do not run very deep: "We are afflicted in every way, but not crushed; perplexed, but not driven to despair..." (4.8). Later on in that same letter, he tells of a strange malady he euphemistically calls "a thorn...in the flesh, a messenger of Satan..." (12.7). He even describes the purpose of this thorn as being to prevent his being "too elated" (12.7). We might wonder about his mood at the time of his repeated prayers for the removal of this thorn. Entering his skin as much as we can, we can well suppose Paul is a man who knows what it means to sink into depression.

Even Jesus himself displayed signs such as these. We cannot let devotion to him blind us from seeing all that was true about him. When, for example, his disciples could not cure a boy brought to them by his father at the foot of the Mount of Transfiguration, Jesus said, "You faithless generation, how much longer must I be among you? How much longer must I put up with you?" (Mk 9.19; cf. Mt 17.17 and Lk 9.41). Whether he was expressing here some kind of frustration over the disciples or over the nuisance of demons, I do not know, but he seems to have had a weariness about something. Whatever this feeling was, it stood in stark contrast to the joy that must have been his atop the mount during the moments of transfiguration.

More poignantly, Jesus confesses to being "deeply grieved" in the Garden of Gethsemane (Mk 13.34). While there are those who believe Jesus' use of Psalm 22.1 upon the cross was a shorthand reference to the entire song, and thus hopeful, others take it at its face value and sense Jesus was dying under the agonizing feeling of godforsakenness. I am referring to his well-known cry from the cross, "My God, my God, why have you forsaken me?" (Mk 15.34 and parallels). The words of Isaiah 53.3, so often applied to Jesus in our liturgies, describe him aptly:

> He was despised and rejected by men;
> a man of sorrows, and acquainted with grief;
> and as one from whom men hide their faces
> he was despised, and we esteemed him not [RSV].

Historical Witness

In addition to biblical testimony regarding depressed persons there is a long record that continues into contemporary times. Many of those who have served in the ranks of the clergy through Christian history experienced periodic bouts with depression, often severe. Remembering these names and recalling these life stories can be helpful in opening up for parishioners a truth about their own pastor, a truth the minister tends to battle secretly and sometimes with shame.

Frederick W. Robertson (1816-1853) is not as widely known today as he was a generation or so ago. From shortly after his death until recent times he was known as a prince among preachers, highly gifted, full of insight, and especially effective in the pulpit. Robertson himself knew none of that. He died young and he died thinking of himself as a failure. Throughout his brief ministerial career he was plagued by depression brought on by feelings of failure that dogged him. One of his biographers reports that Sunday nights and Mondays were the worst. After he exerted himself in the work of the Lord's Day, "moody thoughts drifted in like fog from the sea." These thoughts overtook his dreams. Though he worked hard as a pastor and as a preacher, his despondency focused on imagined work that supposedly went undone. This unfinished business haunted his sleep as he dreamed of parishioners unvisited and people untaught. In his waking hours, he had no idea who these people were; he only knew them in his nightmares. Also stealing into his sleep were dreams of people gossiping about him, his worthless sermons and his sham success. All this made him sick of body as well as soul. He wore out before his time.

Antoinette Brown (1825-1921) was the first woman ordained to Christian ministry in the United States. This occurred on September 15, 1853, in a small Congregational Church in South Butler, New York. As an aside, we can wonder why women were not ordained much earlier. Jesus, it seems to me, gave the precedent for ordaining women as early as the first Easter morning when he told Mary to tell the others he had risen from the dead. Still, Antoinette Brown was a pioneer and many of the women who have succeeded her in ministry feel as though they must be pioneers right up to this day. One of the facts a newly ordained woman has confronting her is that the chances are good she will be the first woman pastor of the church to which she called. This means she will have to break some of the same ground Antoinette Brown had to break more than a hundred years ago.

Congregations who have not had a woman pastor before but do now will be wise to pay attention, for Brown's experience was not good. She pastored the South Butler church only briefly. Exhaustion and depression, together with theological questions about her orthodoxy, led to her resignation in 1854. She thereafter devoted her life to speaking and writing, largely with reference to women's rights, but also to philosophy, religion, and some fiction.

The emotional strain Brown felt in her work at South Butler came from a variety of sources. Among them were the expectations a congregation places upon a pastor, expectations which vary from parishioner to parishioner. Additional pressure came from her feminist friends who did not approve of her career choice. They did not think parish work was conducive to the wider task of changing the status of women in the United States. This left Brown feeling even more isolated in a life that tends to leave one feeling isolated in the first place. On top of all this, theological questions began to rise up within Brown herself, and these put her at odds with the theology she was expected to preach Sunday by Sunday. These theological questions intensified when two children of the parish died. The immediate aftermath for Antoinette Brown was that her own health failed into what she called a "brain fever," and she resigned from the South Butler church.

Harry Emerson Fosdick (1878-1969) suffered a severe breakdown during his seminary years. It is difficult to tell whether this breakdown came as the result of an inherited weak constitution or culture shock brought on by mission work he was doing in the Bowery district. We do know that, whatever the cause, it brought Fosdick to the brink of suicide. His father found him one day with a razor to this throat. His cry of "Harry! Harry!" kept young Fosdick from following through. It was months before he was ready to resume his studies in preparation for ministry. Years later he counseled a fellow clergyman who was experiencing some similar travail. Fosdick told him, no doubt out of his own experience, "Don't let anyone tell you to pull yourself together because what you pull yourself together with is broke."

Andrew W. Blackwood's (1882-1966) emotional health broke twice. The first occurred, like Fosdick's, when he was a seminary student. It led to him transferring schools to be closer to home where he would be nearer to his physician father. The second happened right after he starting teaching at Princeton Theological Seminary. This bout with strain hit harder than the first and lasted longer. It laid him low for over a year.

Another famous preacher to endure such moments was William E. Sangster (1900-1960). Sangster so battled this demon alone that even his wife did not know what was wrong at the time; she only knew something was wrong with her husband. When he died thirty years later, their son was cleaning out Sangster's things. He found a handwritten note in his father's desk drawer. It was written during the time of agony and spelled out inner feelings of defeat and failure. When these feelings were the most severe, they robbed him of zest for work and joy for living.

Our walk through the ministerial hall of fame could continue, pausing by the likes of servants such as Charles Haddon Spurgeon (1834-1892), G. Campbell Morgan (1863-1945), Robert William Dale (1829-1895), and others. The same pall we have been finding in the lives of those already discussed is cast over these as well. It can even be detected in the buoyant Norman Vincent Peale (1898-1993). His positive outlook was blanketed with bleakness not long after he started his long ministry at New York City's Marble Collegiate Church. Apparently the shroud of depression can fall over any ministry.

Local Reality

The chances are quite good your pastor will join the company of those whom this specter visits. Likewise, every time your pastor is haunted by such a demon, the chances are just as good that every attempt will be made to hide the malady from you.

Before proceeding further, however, clarifications are in order. We should distinguish between depression and "the blues." Though neither is fun, the first is much more serious and can require more clinical treatment. Both are conditions of despair, which is the absence of hope. Both interfere with one's ability to be happy, positive, energetic, and creative. Both leave one feeling weary, helpless, and, often, worthless. Additionally, both can make a person irritable, ill, restless and even suicidal. What distinguishes depression from the blues is persistence. It is normal for persons to feel sad or empty following disappointment or loss, but these feelings pass away in time. When the empty mood does not go away, or when it recurs with some degree of frequency, the spells of sadness may be signs of a more serious depression. A fact sheet prepared by the National Alliance for the Mentally Ill indicates that, on average, it takes eight years to get major depression accurately diagnosed. This itself is evidence of the fine line between depression and the blues, and the difficulty of distinguishing one from the other.

One of the inherent risks associated with this lack of a clear differentiation between depression and the blues is that your pastor will likely attempt to treat depression as though it were a minor case of the blues, and will do so no matter how recurrent the feelings of emptiness may be. Typically, a pastor will attempt to overcome the lows with more strenuous prayer. While we do not have all the facts before us, this is apparently what William Sangster's strategy was when he was undergoing his inner turmoil. The note his son found in the desk drawer was a prescription for more prayer and lots of it. Certainly prayer is a good thing, but our hope rests on the one who answers prayer rather than on our efforts as persons of prayer. This is something we know when we are in the sunlight, but, when we are under ominous clouds the true nature of our hope is obscured. If and when this happens to your minister, the chances are that he or she will be wrestling in prayer and agonizing over the fact that the prayers being said are not bringing him or her out of the doldrums. That will only drive him or her to more prayer which will play out as more frustration with the self as someone who is either not capable of praying well or not deserving of a happier answer.

The pattern should be obvious. It is obvious, but only to those who are not depressed or otherwise sunk low. The more depressed we are, the more we want to recoup our hope because hope is what is lost. The more spiritually minded we are, the more we seek to recoup our hope through our abilities to be spiritual. We put trust in our abilities because, in the midst of depression, we do not think we have anything else. The more our abilities fail us, the more hope we lose. The more hope we lose, the further we sink into depression.

Among ministers, these attempts to cure one's own depression through more strenuous prayer coincide with feelings of incredible guilt. New ministers especially, that is persons who have never experienced the occupational hazard that ministerial blues seem to be and who are not aware that colleagues undergo similar predicaments, are susceptible to the salt of guilt being poured into the wounds of depression. Here the thinking is that we are spiritual people and are even called to be models of the devotional life. We want to be perceived as being successful and whole. We want to be respected as men and women of God, leaders who know how to draw deeply from scripture, the resources of grace, and the wells of salvation. But we are at a loss when the devotional life does not seem to be working for us and we fear exposure. If the curtain were pulled back, we suppose, we would be seen as shams, castaways, hypocrites. As a result, clergy battle depression secretly and alone, not wanting parishioners or colleagues to know of their emptiness and inner struggle. William Sangster's aloneness was so acute that even his wife did not know its details or depths.

It should be apparent that there are dangers pursuant to these moods of depression and their consequent feelings of guilt. The first danger is suicide. Fosdick was at the very brink of it before his father stopped him. Suicide is not a sin. It is a tragedy. It is the last resort of a broken soul, perhaps loathsome to itself and certainly, at least as far as it can tell, alienated from its hope. Those who survive will see it for the sad, and perhaps selfish, act it was and they will wish the one who is gone could have seen life for what it really had in store.

Another danger is physical collapse. This is the breakdown of health. One of the great mysteries of life is the close relationship between body and spirit. One affects the other. Each is somehow dependent upon the other. Those whose spirits are broken are susceptible to sickness. In these cases it can be said the sickness is not "all in their heads" but all in their hearts. A lackluster spirit makes a body easy prey for viruses and other maladies. Likewise this same cheerlessness slows healing. Recognizing this, the aforementioned fact sheet prepared by the National Alliance for the Mentally Ill includes, as a possible diagnostic indicator of major depression, physical disorders that persist and do not respond to treatment.

Moral crisis needs to be mentioned as a danger, too. Sexual misconduct, malfeasance with regard to money, and other forms of inappropriate behavior can be traced to depression misdiagnosed and mishandled. A good person in the throes of something perceived to be threatening and dreadful can make poor decisions, even ones contrary to their better ideals. Wrongdoing can be more an act of desperation than of overt disobedience. Those of us who have not been as far as this precipice can wonder why a person with so much going for him or her would risk throwing it all away. It could be that the answer is to be found in the fact that the person with everything was in a state of hopelessness and convinced they had nothing to lose.

The final danger to mention is perhaps more subtle and widespread among clergy than suicide, physical illness brought on by depression, and moral crisis precipitated by despondency. This danger can go by the broad umbrella term of changed personality. Depression can manifest itself in a variety of ways including cynicism, a hardened heart, an angry tone, a sarcastic wit, a lethargic spirit, and more. Any one of these can lead a person to act out in manners detrimental and destructive to ministry.

Root Causes

I suspect many of you would have never thought depression would be such a severe or widespread problem among clergy. This brings us to the question that has no doubt been long on your mind throughout this chapter. Can it really be as bad as it sounds? What on earth do *ministers* have to be depressed about? Frankly, the better the church, the less there is to be depressed about. But depression is possible in even good churches. Why?

One reason is because ministry is such a massive task. John Calvin called the parish pastor absolutely pivotal to the life of the church. He was right, but that is a bane as well as a blessing. The blessing is to be found in the opportunities it provides us to equip the church, strengthen the saints, and engage in mission under God. The bane is to be found in the heavy responsibilities associated with the pastoral office. Even though the church is replete with capable lay officers and workers, the minister is it seems, on the human level, the one where the buck stops. The minister is the up front person, to "go to" guy or gal, around whom the church seems to gather and pick up steam, again on the human level. To always be in this lead role is draining. The feeling of responsibility can be overwhelming. This makes clergy easy targets for depression.

Related to this is the burden of unfinished business. This is what took a terrible toll on Frederick W. Robertson. He was extremely faithful in his work and effective in his preaching and teaching, but he was ever conscious of work undone. Two things feed into a minister's sorrow here. One is the constant neediness that is around us, and the other is the time clock that is never around for us to "punch out" for the day. Through no fault of their own, our people are nearly always in a position that could call for a pastoral response. Whether we are thinking of seasons of joy or pain, there is always someone with whom we could weep, rejoice, pray or sit. And, by nature of the relentless pace at which Sundays roll around, there is always the pulpit demanding that we prepare for it by way of prayer and study. It seems silly to say this, but it is true: a minister's work - and, more importantly, what the public perceives to be the minister's work - is never done. There is always something to do. With no time clock around, and with the perception that ministers are on 24-hour-call, there is little sense of being off duty. This is fertile ground for the weariness where depression grows best.

We can add to the burden of unfinished business the lack of noticeable results. Jesus spoke of the realm of God in terms of seeds being sown. These seeds will eventually produce a full and abundant harvest. But between the sowing and the harvesting the field still looks pretty empty. The harvest we are promised is, faith tells us, inevitable. That is good. It is not, however, immediate. That is a source of ministerial despair. We can put in a full day's work but have nothing visible to show for it at the end of the day. We cannot look back and see that anything was accomplished.

This is burdensome enough in regular circumstances, but it becomes even more troublesome to the pastoral soul who lives and works among a results-oriented people. The leaders in a church may be, let us say, leaders in local business. Their attention throughout the work-week is on meeting goals, achieving priorities, showing profits, and so forth. They may be ready to hold their pastor to the same kind of accountability, or the pastor may think they are ready to hold him or her to the same measurable standards of success. Sadly, pastors come to the Council or Consistory meetings with tally sheets indicating the number of calls, hospital visits, and other pastoral contacts that have occurred since the last meeting. I judge this to be an attempt to justify ministry according to the standards of another profession or occupation, and I judge it to be either despondency in action or depression in the making. Our work simply cannot be tallied. To do work that cannot be tallied in a tallying world is to do a work that takes a toll on the soul.

Petty complaining leads to ministerial depression. One complaint, however minor, can undercut any number of compliments, however grand. Look again at the tally sheet brought to the Consistory meeting. The pastor can be thinking the numbers look good, but a single comment about the parsonage lawn or backyard hedge can undo it all. I distinctly recall one Easter morning. The house was packed, the sermon went well, the lilies were beautiful, the choir music was grand, and the congregational singing was powerful. As the parishioners filed by me on their way out of the sanctuary, their smiles were broad, their faces were beaming, and there was a steady stream of compliments and words of appreciation over the service. Then along came some man I did not know, the visiting brother of a parishioner. His remark? Not about the music, the sermon, the lilies, the attendance, or even the Christ. It was about the flag. For him, the gold fringe sewn on the American flag made it satanic. I told him I had never heard that before, and I asked him to send me some literature. He never did. I never recovered the buoyant Easter spirit I had had up until that point.

There is not a lot ministers can do about this petty complaining. There was murmuring against Moses not long after the congregation of the Exodus left Egypt, so I suspect there will murmuring against ministers and congregations as long as pastoral offices are filled and church doors are open. It is something we have to contend with, like it or not. Some of it can be laughed off. Some of it can be shrugged off. Some of it hits deeper and cannot be easily dismissed. Clergy are not in a position to respond in kind. People may like sermons warning about hell, but they don't like us to tell them to go there. Petty complaints that hit deep hurt and we cannot respond out of the real emotion we feel. We cannot lash out, so anger gets sucked in. This internalized anger that has no safe context for expression manifests itself as depression.

Clergy finances will be the subject of the next chapter, but we can say here that this, too, is a cause for depression among pastors. This is particularly true for the first church, which is often a first church because it cannot or will not afford to call experienced pastors into their service. It does not matter that Christian tradition thinks of envy as one of the seven deadly sins. Pastors are not immune to it. I am the first to arrive in our parking lot on Sunday mornings and the last to leave. Sometimes I wonder if that is not a secret coping mechanism against the evils of envy. I do not want to see the cars my parishioners drive, so I stay away from the parking lot when they are there. And this says nothing about the houses in which they live! My salary is not pitiful, but my heart is not free from envy, either. I hate admitting this to myself, much less to my parishioners. As a result, it never gets voiced in the light of day. The result is that internalized envy, like internalized anger, manifests itself in depression.

Now that you know pastors are quite susceptible to conditions of deep depression as well as minor cases of the blues, you are in a better position to care for your pastor on a spiritual and emotional level. I hasten to add, however, that what you as an individual or your congregation as a community does with this knowledge about clergy depression depends upon your pastor. Remember that clergy feel vulnerable not only to depression but also to a certain guilt when they are depressed. To be reminded that you know they are depressed may be depressing in itself. What are you to do?

Perhaps the best course of action is for you to turn this knowledge into an increased incentive to pray for your pastor and set picks like an ally. The most a congregation has control over is the petty complaining. This may never be stopped but it can be slowed or deflected away from the pastor. Lay people are in a better position, especially early in a minister's pastorate, to put other lay people on notice that their complaints are petty and unnecessary. If you have been part of your church for any period of time, you know who these people are. The young pastor may not know everybody in the church laughs off Mrs. B's complaining and shrugs off Mr. G's gruff criticisms. If you help the pastor know that, and if you publicly laugh off Mrs. B and shrug off Mr. G, three people will learn important lessons: Mrs. B., Mr. G., and your new Rev. It is unlikely the rebuff will make the first two depressed, but it is likely it will keep the third from becoming depressed. And you will have served the kingdom.

Chapter Five

What Income the Minister Should Receive

"Few readers of these lines will start on as tiny a salary as we two. In a day when a dollar went farther than now, we began with eight hundred dollars and a manse, part of which my husband had already furnished. We bought only two pieces of furniture new, a cookstove and a china cabinet in which to display our wedding gifts. Everything else came in as 'used furniture.' I gave piano lessons at fifty cents apiece and made five dollars a week. We managed to keep our heads above water, and in normal times we actually saved a part of the salary! However, in December I had an operation, which wiped out our furniture fund. Se we had to begin again from scratch."

Those are the words of Carolyn P. Blackwood, wife of Andrew W. Blackwood, and they are from her now very dated book [*The Pastor's Wife* (Philadelphia: The Westminster Press, 1951), p. 77]. The Blackwoods were married in 1910, nearly two years after Andrew's ordination, and this parsonage Mrs. Blackwood mentions was in Walton, Kansas. Times have changed indeed, but facts remain largely the same. Individual circumstances are different now than they were in 1910, but the underlying conditions of the Blackwoods' experience in Kansas still prevail. More often than not, first churches are first churches because they cannot or will not afford to offer a larger salary complete with benefits.

When it comes to the question of how much money a minister should receive, in an entry level church or any other, it is difficult to assign a dollar figure. The cost of living varies from region to region across the United States. What is a large salary in part of the country may be quite low when matched against the expenses of living in another part. A friend of mine, now retired and living in the Pacific Northwest, tells of a ministerial candidate who turned down a call to serve the church my friend attends because the salary offer was nowhere near what the candidate was already earning from a congregation in a large city closer to the Atlantic. If measured by a keen eye, sharp enough to notice cost of living differentials, the salaries may have been quite comparable. Since my eye is not that sharp, and since I hope my readership is widespread, I'll not offer any dollar figures as to the minimum a new pastor should receive.

There is one rule of thumb, however, that seems to apply to all parts of the United States as well as to all parts of Christ's Church. That rule is this:

Congregations should pay their ministers as much as they can. A corollary adds that this means most congregations should pay more than they do. Clergy salaries have never been high when compared to the earnings of persons with comparable education and demands placed upon their time. We who are on the receiving end of these salaries can sometimes feel as though this is used as an excuse to keep them low. My purpose here is to strive to convince you to keep your pastor's salary high and to look for ways to increase it.

The Need for a Reasonable Salary

It is easy enough to make the case that every congregation should offer its pastor reasonable and generous compensation. We can begin to build the foundation for this case by turning to scripture. Among the most direct biblical references to clergy compensation is 1 Timothy 5.17-18. There we read, "Let the elders who rule well be considered worthy of a double honor, especially those who labor in preaching and teaching; for the scripture says, 'You shall not muzzle an ox while it is treading out the grain,' and, 'The laborer deserves to be paid.'"

The Apostle Paul, it would seem, did not himself accept remuneration from the churches under his charge. In Corinth, for example, he worked, together with Aquila, as a tentmaker at least part of the time (Acts 18.1-4; 2 Cor. 11.7-9). He seems to have adopted the same practice in Thessalonica (2 Thess. 3.7-9). This is the source of the term *tentmaking ministry*. One who serves in this capacity relies upon some other occupation in order to make a living, but pastors a church or performs some other ministry on a part-time basis. There may be some compensation received from the church, but this is not the tentmaker's sole means of support.

This practice notwithstanding, Paul is nonetheless adamant that he would have been well within his rights as an apostle to accept a salary. He speaks at length, comparing ministry with other occupations, and insists that clergy, too, deserve to be paid for what they do:

> Do we not have the right to our food and drink? Do we not have the right to be accompanied by a believing wife, as do other apostles and the brothers of the Lord and Cephas? Or is it only Barnabas and I who have no right to refrain from working for a living? Who at any time pays the expenses for doing military service? Who plants a vineyard and does not eat any of its fruit? Or who tends a flock and does not get any of its milk? (1 Cor. 9.4-7)

Paul moves on to base this claim in scripture, using the same Old Testament text mentioned in 1 Timothy 5.18:

> Do I say this on human authority? Does not the law also say the

same? For it is written in the law of Moses, "You shall not muzzle an ox while it is treading out the grain." Is it for oxen that God is concerned? Or does he not speak entirely for our sake? It was indeed written for our sake, for whoever plows should plow in hope and whoever threshes should thresh in hope of a share in the crop. If we have sown spiritual good among you, is it too much if we reap your material benefits? (1 Cor. 9.8-12a)

He brings his case to a close by referring to temple servants and the command of the Lord:

Do you not know that those who are employed in the temple service get their food from the temple, and those who serve at the altar share in what is sacrificed on the altar? In the same way, the Lord commanded that those who proclaim the gospel should get their living by the gospel. (1 Cor. 9.13-14)

When Jesus sent out the seventy two by two, he expected them to rely upon those whom they served for their needs. They were not to be encumbered by much themselves. They were to rely upon the hospitality of those who accepted them. Jesus' instructions included the words, "Remain in the same house, eating and drinking whatever they provide, for the laborer deserves to be paid" (Luke 10.7). 1 Timothy 5.18, as we have already seen, drew upon this last phrase, reiterating it with reference to clergy compensation. We should note that the Lord's remark speaks to the providers as much as it does to the recipients. The seventy are to accept what they are offered, for they deserve to receive, and persons in the towns to which they go should provide something, again because these missionaries are deserving. Thus, there should be no qualms about accepting a salary and no reluctance to offer one.

As we have seen, many of these New Testament texts rely upon Deuteronomy 25.4: "You shall not muzzle an on while it is treading out the grain." This rather straightforward law indicates how providing an adequate salary is a justice issue and not simply a biblical requirement. The Old Testament is here recognizing it is cruel to make an animal work without adequate food throughout the day.

This agricultural imagery calls to mind stories I heard in my youth. Though I spent the first part of my childhood on a farm, my father's early death meant that we three who remained were no longer active farmers ourselves. Still, I have been around farmers my whole life. Many of the older ones are able to tell of legendary cheapskates who hired extra hands for room and board, but did not offer much of either. The meager meals at these places became the stuff of neighborhood gossip. The hired help on these farms, whether they were men who worked in the field and barn or women who worked in the house and garden, felt like muzzled oxen, cheated out of a fair day's pay for a fair day's work.

Some churches have the same penny-pinching ways. Before I moved into my second pastorate I was interviewed by another church in another state. My wife and I were met at our hotel by some very cordial people and then given the grand tour of the community. It was a beautiful community, to say the least, and our tour guides pointed out the homes of parishioners along the way. Many of the houses were new and even the older ones were all nice, neat and attractive. The tour ended at the parsonage. If I had had backbone, the interview would have ended then and there, too. It was an absolute eyesore! It needed several coats of paint inside and out, and both of us could spot major repairs that needed to be made. The discrepancies between the houses of the parishioners and the home of the pastor were stark. It seemed to us that a congregation unaware of these discrepancies or, if aware, unembarrassed by them, when attempting to attract a new pastor would quickly neglect the needs of the one called once he or she arrived. I followed through with the interview process only because arrangements had been made for a neutral pulpit the next day, which was Sunday, and I did not want to put that neutral church at a disadvantage. Still, Sherrol and I were certain we were not moving to this church that seemed to promise only a muzzle in the future.

We two think of our brief experience with this church as somewhat comical. It stops being funny, however, when we think of pastors and their families actually living and working under such conditions. The issue is not paint for the parsonage's exterior so much as it is the inner attitudes of the people of the parish. They are not acting with justice when they offer their ministers an inferior salary and keep them in substandard housing. It is not only not funny, it is unholy and should be unacceptable.

Along with being biblical and just, reasonable salaries are, of course, welcome! We who pursue ordained ministry obviously do not get into it for the money. Still, it costs money to enter the field. The first church we serve does not bear the responsibility of supplying the cost of our education, but it needs to be aware we are still paying for our education. No doubt this true for anyone who takes a first job fresh out of school, no matter the field. Physicians, lawyers, bankers, teachers - all must pay for their college and graduate school work. Ministers are not unique in this. The chief difference lies in the fact that clergy salaries tend to be significantly and notoriously lower than in these other fields, making repayment of college and seminary loans slower and more burdensome.

I was ordained in 1982 and commenced serving a church at a salary of $12,500 plus parsonage. Inheritances and money saved from summer jobs had paid for my undergraduate education, but my seminary bills remained. The car I had been driving through college and seminary years was no longer reliable and needed to be replaced. Sherrol and I were married in 1983, but our situation was such that we could not expect any help from our parents in financing our wedding. We did that on our own. Our first little one arrived in the late summer of 1984, and the other two came in 1986 and 1987. The details escape me now, but the insurance we had then was pretty short-armed when it came to reaching out with benefits, and the pediatrician bills, even for "healthy baby" visits, mounted up quickly. All this while, we were living on my salary alone. We could barely afford maternity clothes for one of Sherrol's pregnancies, and finding money to put gas in the car meant relying on the grace of God. The people of the church were warm and generous, but funds were tight all the way around. They were doing the best they could, and so were we. The directors of one of the local funeral homes befriended me, and called upon my services to minister to families who had no other connection with clergy. These funerals, and an occasional wedding, seemed to come just when we needed extra funds.

Again, a new pastor's seminary debt is not the church's responsibility. Perhaps it should become *the denomination's* responsibility in some shared way with the pastor, but the congregation should not be expected to pay these bills. Nevertheless, the first church does need to keep in mind that their new pastor is under this kind of financial burden. Likewise, it needs to bear in mind that the pastor is a public person and all the others in the pastor's family join him or her in being so. The car they drive, the clothes they wear, and so forth, are part of their public image. Most of us are not interested in being fashion mongers, but we do not want to be embarrassed by our appearance, either. The sad fact is that many of us, when we start, are expected to project a certain image in the community but we do not have from our churches the financial wherewithal to do so. This in turn opens us, or members of our families, to petty complaints.

The Need for Stewardship Education

The typical church will agree with everything that has been said so far and own the importance and desirability of providing pastors with a reasonable salary. But this same church will wonder how it can be done. Someone, at some point during the budget discussion when salaries are fixed, will say to their pastoral friend, "This is less than you deserve, and we wish we could offer you more; but this is the best we can do this year." If this statement is really meant and is not simply a smokescreen, then something needs to be done to put the congregation in a better position to offer the higher salary. The only place to begin is with the people who are part of the congregation now and to start them on a course of stewardship education.

Realistically, the chances are good attendance will be bad at a formal class on stewardship which your pastor might teach. A Disciples of Christ minister is convinced that 20% of the people who are normally present on a Sunday morning will absent themselves from the sanctuary when they know the sermon will be on stewardship. Your own congregation's attempts to highlight a Stewardship Sunday may have proved this statistic to be true. At any rate, few congregations, if any, can count on sizable attendance at a special Bible study or other class on this theme. Thus, your pastor may not have the best opportunities to do much stewardship teaching directly. You, however, can conduct much of this work indirectly by the way you talk about money matters in your conversations in and around the church.

You can promote better stewardship in your church by speaking openly about money. Some congregations tend to treat money as a subject more taboo than sex. To give them the benefit of the doubt, they are afraid the church will be accused of talking only about money, so they never talk about money. More cynically, some of us suspect they do not want to talk about money because they do not want to part with it, and they are afraid they will have to if Christ's church begins to make a claim on it. Somehow the idea has gotten around that it is impolite for the church to discuss money, so a vast number of congregations hesitate to broach the subject with their people. The truth of the matter is that it is never impolite to discuss any subject the Bible discusses openly and treats as important. Money matters fall into this category. Jesus talked of money often. So did Paul and the rest of the New Testament. To listen to voices which say we should not talk of such things in the church is to listen to voices that are sub-Christian in their origin, orientation and outlook. You can do much to promote stewardship in your congregation by gently countering these voices whenever they are heard.

As you have opportunity, you can promote stewardship in your congregation by speaking about giving as a way of worshiping God. The offering that is taken on Sunday morning is an act of worship. It is an expression of love for and gratitude to God. It is a pledge of one's self - heart, soul, mind and strength - to the cause of Christ. One of our chief difficulties, however, is that, outside the sanctuary, we speak of the offering as a business transaction rather than as an act of worship. It is treated as fund raising. It is paying the light bill. It is supporting the budget. It is seen less as a gift to God than as an obligation to the utility company. We cannot ignore the practicalities which indicate quite clearly that the money collected pays church bills, but if this is the language we use toward the justification of the offering, we have turned our faith upside down and inside out. It makes it seem as though the great God of Creation is a pauper who must beg. The more we speak of the offering as what the church needs, the more God as the Great Provider falls from the picture. On the other hand, the more we speak of God as the Great Provider, the more we seem to have. Above all, we begin to see that, under this God, every church has all that it needs to accomplish the purpose God ordains for it. You can do much to transform your congregation's attitude toward stewardship by speaking more of the blessings God has provided, blessings which call for gratitude and praise expressed tangibly.

Similarly, you can improve your congregation's attitude toward stewardship by talking of giving as a joyful exercise. Nearly everyone knows and can quote this verse from 2 Corinthians: "Each of you must give as you have made up your mind, not reluctantly or under compulsion, for God loves a cheerful giver" (9.7). It would be nice if it were more widely known that the Greek word translated here as *cheerful* is related to our word *hilarious* and could be translated as such. "God loves a hilarious giver!" I once heard a speaker who returned from Ghana say that the Christians he met in that African country actually gave that way - each worshiper sang and danced as he or she brought a gift to the front of the church. Most folks I know seem pretty quiet during the offering and solemnly watch the plate go from person to person, each one glad they did not drop it, and each one seeming to do their best to hide the amount they give by wadding up the bills or making sure the envelope is upside down. If anyone is singing, it is the choir - probably because the plate is not passed to them during an anthem! - and absolutely no one is dancing.

All kidding aside, while there does not seem to be much joy at the moment of our giving, it strikes me that the people of our churches do love to give. Additionally, the more we tell them they love to give, the more they begin to think that themselves. Similarly, the more we whine at people for not giving, the more reluctant they become to dignify our requests with a generous response. The more we ask in a measly way, they less they will give in a generous way. You can do much to transform your congregation's stewardship by highlighting this "giving until it feels good" as opposed to some "give until it hurts" strategy. No one wants to hurt; everyone wants to feel good. If we try to tap into people's joy more than we try to reach into their wallets, the chances are they will become - maybe not phenomenal, but at least - better stewards, more closely approximating the cheerful givers who are not reluctant or under compulsion.

The Need for Help with Negotiation

Advocates for better stewardship put the church in a position to offer the minister a higher salary and they enhance the spirit and work of the entire congregation. No church can have enough of these kinds of people. Nevertheless, no matter how many of these advocates there may be, there is yet room for pastoral allies who negotiate on the minister's behalf. We should not think of these along the same lines as we do those agents who help professional athletes sign lucrative contracts for exorbitant amounts, taking a sizable cut themselves. Instead we should think of them as people who care for the life and ministry of the church. They are friends who want to help a process that is awkward at best be handled as smoothly and fairly as possible. In some settings, this work may fall to the Pastoral Relations Committee, but it will take the new pastor a while to develop such a committee complete with all the trust this sensitive panel requires.

Like it or not, salary negotiations pit pastors against congregations on an annual basis. This occurs every year even in the best of congregations with the best of pastoral relationships. We do not seem to handle this very well. Many of us in the clergy are, for a variety of reasons, timid when it comes to asking for money for ourselves. We do not like negotiating because we do not want to be the issue. Knowing full well that the lion's share of the church's budget will go to clergy salary, and sensing how hard it is for the people to meet that budget every year, we are reluctant to ask them to give even more to us.

Basing a request for a raise on accomplishments we have achieved does not seem right, either. Listing accomplishments as if they were my achievements, and using them as leverage toward a higher salary, does not seem to me to be the church's way of working, and it is not mine. If I allowed myself to think and act that way, something in my self-understanding as a minister would have to give way, and I am not prepared for that to happen.

Besides, if I try to ask for a raise on the basis of merit, I raise the subject of clergy evaluation and that is not subject I like anyone to dwell upon. I am enough like Paul to realize I am not the man I want to be; the good I want I do not do. Whatever there is that may be meritorious in my work is more than matched by pieces of it that are dubious. If I ask for a raise, the truth may come out that I do not deserve one; if I keep my mouth shut, I may get one and be all right until next year.

The lay people of the church are just as uncomfortable with salary negotiations as are their pastors. Someone who is on a Church Council, let us say, may never be in a position in their secular life where they have to negotiate salary. If this person is on the earning side of a salary, it could be that someone from the union does the negotiating or it could be they are self-employed. The point is they themselves never have to ask for a raise; the pay scale at the place of employment is set and raises occur on a fixed schedule never open to question. Salary negotiation puts this poor soul in a strange new territory; he or she may want to do right but not have the slightest idea as to where to begin.

According to another set of circumstances, our hypothetical Council member could be, in his or her secular life, on the management side of salary negotiations. This experience may be perceived to be helpful, but it can actually get in the way. The standards used in the secular workplace are not easily transferred to the church. I heard of one congregation that told its minister there would be increases in salary if certain criteria were met within the next several months. No doubt, the person heading the negotiations for the church thought of these as incentives for increased effort and productivity. This may be appropriate for people in some kind of sales force, but the church and its ministry simply cannot accept a standard of this nature. Clergy compensation cannot be determined on a commission basis that allows increases based on worship attendance figures, the number of pastoral calls, or new members received. Ministry is not piece work. It is not sales. It is not business.

Since negotiating is awkward at best for pastor and laity alike, and since the pastor is often alone in trying to make the case that ministry patterns and business principles are separate and distinct realities, many pastors would welcome allies in the negotiating process. Whether these allies take a formal or informal role is less important than their ability to help set the terms of the discussion among their brothers and sisters in the church. Like stewardship advocates who set the tone for better stewardship by the way they speak about giving during the course of their lives in the congregation, allies in negotiation exemplify a different way of looking at pastoral salaries. These allies begin to open eyes by speaking of the church as different from a business and by naming that the church ought to have a different standard than the world for determining increases.

Allies in negotiation know the difference between a pastor's base salary - what the minister gets - and the total package - which is what it costs the church to have a minister. All too often it seems, folks look at the church budget at congregational meetings, see the total package - which includes mileage, insurances, Social Security offsets, continuing education provisions, book allowances, and incidental expenses - and think this is what they pay their minister. In actuality, this is what it costs the church to have a minister.

Allies of this nature are also aware that there are Conference guidelines for determining ministerial salaries. Each year, the Wisconsin Conference of the United Church of Christ sends two copies of its set of guidelines to every one of its congregations. One copy is for the pastor and one is for the lay committee responsible for working with the pastor to determine salary. Other Conferences of our denomination do much the same. Individual congregations may not be able to meet these standards, but it is helpful to them and to pastors to know that these standards exist, if only to provide a church-related model for determining salary. Additionally, if there is at least one person in the congregation other than the minister who knows about Conference guidelinend as is vocal about them, this can disarm an individual who may be attempting to wield inordinate power around clergy salary.

The most savvy of allies will check with their pastor's spouse around the time the salary is set. The spouse may or may not feel comfortable making any suggestions, but he or she will appreciate being asked. Every marriage finds its own way of structuring its life. In our household, for example, Sherrol manages our finances. She has a better sense of what our family requires financially than I do.

The Need for a Long Vacation

Salary negotiation includes coming to an agreement as to the amount of vacation time a pastor is allowed. Alexander Whyte (1836-1921), a powerhouse preacher from Scotland, was well known in his day for being an advocate of long vacations for pastors. He himself enjoyed at least two months in the summer and additional time at other points in the year! It should be noted, however, that Whyte's time away from his pastorate in the city of Edinburgh was not time away from work. A veritable library went along with him on these holidays, and he worked at a desk or table for hours each day, preparing for the preaching and teaching that would occupy the months ahead.

I have neither the courage nor the inclination to call for the amount of vacation time Whyte did, but I do believe every pastor - and this includes beginning pastors - should be allowed no less than four weeks of vacation every year. This suggestion may startle or even offend lay people who have to work long years at their place of employment before they receive as many as two weeks of vacation time. How is it that a new pastor deserves at least four weeks?

The rationale for long ministerial vacations is found in the nature of ministry itself. Our work may not be physically demanding, but it is emotionally, spiritually and intellectually draining. Sufficient rest is needed if one is to have the power to continue. Other workers have the blessing of the weekend, and they use these days off for rest, recreation, work around the house or some other such activity that is a change of pace and scenery from the workaday world. Clergy obviously do not have their weekends free. They may jealously guard a day off every week, and rightly so, but two days side by side are extremely hard to come by. Often the one we try to guard is claimed by some legitimate cause in and for the church. It is not ideal, but it is also not unusual, for pastors to go stretches at a time, perhaps a month or more, with only one day off. A generous vacation, which allows sufficient time for the minister to get away from the church and, preferably, out of town, is the best way to build significant and necessary periods of sabbath rest into a pastor's life.

Some clergy like to divide their vacation time, taking a week here and there at various points throughout the year. My own preference has been to take all my vacation time at once. Since we have lived our entire married life in the Midwest, and my wife's parents and siblings, and our children's only cousins, have lived two thousand miles away in the Pacific Northwest, and since we could little afford to fly one of us there much less five, the full month at a time has been necessary to allow for the cross country drive as well as the visit with relatives. We have tried, especially when the children were little, to make that trip every other year. The "off year," as we called it, was spent at home, often doing some repair project on the house or in the yard. Though I am no Alexander Whyte, I would like to add that, whether home or away, books have been my vacation companions, meaning the month always carried some freight for the church.

The churches I have served have never grumbled about this month away. If there is a drawback, it is that worship attendance suffers. It seems that worship attendance is always a bit lower in the summer and drops off somewhat markedly when the pastor is away. This is, of course, not right, but it is not the minister's fault! The pastor should not be denied a good vacation because the people will not come if he or she is gone. We should help our people realize that the Lord knows if they are in church even though they think they are getting away with something when the pastor is not looking!

The Need for Comfortable Housing

More important than a sizeable vacation is comfortable housing. It is more important because your pastor and his or her family will spend more time at home than they will on vacation. If a church meeting ever has the feeling of a hornet's nest, there is nothing like coming home to a place of quiet rest. As for what is meant by the term *comfortable housing*, I would define it as any place the people of the church would be proud to own and happy to live in themselves.

A welcome trend is for churches to offer a housing allowance as opposed to a parsonage. The advantages of this are three, with the first being most important. That is to say, home ownership allows the pastor to accrue some equity. This can help ministers build toward a better retirement as well as put them in the position of being eligible for a home equity loan, if needed.

Secondly, home ownership as opposed to parsonage living keeps home life separate and distinct from church roles. This of course puts the burden of responsibility for home maintenance on the pastoral family rather than on the shoulders of the Board of Trustees, but, all things considered, I prefer this arrangement of not having church members as landlords. We lived in a parsonage in our first setting and in our own home in the second. Household repairs have been problematic in this second situation because we have had to afford them ourselves when they were necessary. Given my lack of skills in this regard, this has almost always meant hiring the work done. Sometimes I become wistful for the early days when we did not have to afford home maintenance costs or figure out how repairs were to be done; everything was taken care of by members of the congregation. Those members were fine men who like working together and who enjoyed playing with our children, letting them "help" as they worked. I would not trade those days for anything; nevertheless, we felt a certain freedom when we no longer had to go to our church people with this or that malfunction.

Thirdly, parsonages tend to be in close proximity to their churches. This was a decided boon to us during the days in which we were a one-car family who had difficulty finding the cash to fuel that one car. Sherrol did not work outside the home when our children were very little, and I could walk to work. Consequently, our car did not have to be driven much and it was easy to divide its use between the two of us. Given this, I cannot deny that living next door to the church was a blessing; still, it was annoying at times, too. Work was never far away. The church was outside every window on the south side of the house. We had a tiny backyard that was in full view of the church parking lot. I am not sure we had anything to hide, but I am not sure we wanted to be seen, either. In our current situation we are some blocks from the church, and this distance still feels good.

There is a decided disadvantage to giving up the parsonage for the sake of a housing allowance, and this disadvantage comes into play during periods of ministerial transition. Moving is easy when the move is from parsonage to parsonage. No one has to hope a house will sell. No one has to fear an offer will fall through or financing will be denied. Cost of living differentials between two parts of the country are less of a concern when one does not have to worry about rental fees or mortgage payments. Since first pastorates tend to be shorter than later ones, it may be wise for an entry level church to keep its parsonage. This will not in itself prevent the possibility of a longer pastorate, but it will easily accommodate the potential of rather frequent transitions.

Those who dwell in parsonages need to know the space is theirs. I arrived at my first church single and Sherrol and I were married a year later. The search committee and other representatives from the congregation who were making the parsonage ready for my arrival asked a series of good questions. I gave a series of bad answers, and Sherrol paid the price. This is one of my regrets. The questions all had to do with paint, carpet, drapes, and the like. The people were ready to make the church's parsonage my home, and they wanted to know about colors and tastes. I had been living in dormitories at college and seminary for eight years, and I border on being color-blind. I did not know what answers to give to the questions my new friends were asking. I was sure anything would be better than a dorm and that their choice of colors would be fine with me. This worked well for me on the 1st of June when I started living in the parsonage, but it did not work as well for Sherrol when we were married on the 18th of the following June and she started living in it, too. Bless her heart, she accepted what she found but did not have any real say in decorating the first home of her married life. Since we were at that church for nine years, in time there was opportunity to replace with paint the wallpaper she never liked and to change some colors here and there, but she did not have a real chance to make a home hers until we moved to where we are now. The point is, the congregation did the right thing by asking about colors and drapes. It wasn't their fault I had no taste!

But doesn't the Search Committee want the parsonage to be in tip-top shape when they are attracting and interviewing candidates? You cannot show a house badly in need of paint and expect success when it comes to snagging a new minister. Isn't it costly to put on fresh paint today only to change the colors in a few months' time when the new residents arrive? Yes, it is; but this is perhaps the price the church has to pay for not keeping the house well-maintained and attractive

54

during the former pastor's stay.

The parsonage family needs to know the house is theirs from basement to garret. This means church belongings should not be stored there or in the parsonage garage. It means parsonage rooms should not be used for church meetings of any kind unless at the invitation of the minister or minister's spouse. It means no one should have a key to the place or be allowed access to it as though it were community property. Certainly it is community property but it must be regarded as private and personal space. If someone from the church needs a key for reasons related to maintenance and oversight, even this key should be used reluctantly and only with the permission of the pastor or spouse. Let a form of the Golden Rule apply: Treat the minister's house as you would have your own home treated by others.

Other Needs

There are some other income-related needs. These are not part of the base salary but of the total package. As such, they are part of what it costs the church to maintain a pastor. We can simply name these without saying much about any one of them.

There is the need for adequate insurance. Everyone knows from their own experience how necessary health insurance, including dental, is to a family's life. One of the best ways a congregation can care for a pastor is to make sure the insurance provided is the best possible. In the majority of cases, pastors participate in a group plan organized by their Conference or other judicatory. These larger church bodies have, I think, the responsibility of securing the best plans for the pastors with which they are related. Congregations, at least through their official boards, should know about their judicatory's plan and make their premium payments on time.

There is a need for a generous book allowance. I had one in my first church, but I hesitated to use it. I felt a bit selfish asking the church to pay for books I wanted to read. I thought paying for them myself was a way to save the church money. Then the Moderator of the congregation told me one day the church *wanted* me to use this money. This Moderator was a carpenter, and he spoke of my books as comparable to his tools. He helped me see the church people knew I needed them in order to build the sermons I was called to preach. He helped me realize that providing these tools is a necessary church expense.

There is a need for a wedding policy. Those of us who have trouble negotiating salary have a devil of a time charging a fee for services rendered. Weddings fall into this category. When the wedding is for the son or daughter of an active church member, participating in it as the pastor is a joyous privilege. When the wedding is for someone else, especially for someone not related to the church, these services can be little more than a lot of work. Above all, they take time away from family, occupying a Friday night for rehearsal and Saturday for the wedding. The wedding may be in the middle of the day, but it occupies the entire day. Your pastor may not feel right about charging a fee to an active member; opinions differ as to whether or not this should occur. However, the church must help and support the pastor in setting a reasonable fee for others, especially if the congregation wants the minister to do the weddings of nonmembers as an outreach ministry. A sad fact is that there seem to be people who throw expensive weddings to impress their friends and families but try to cut their expenses when it comes to the minister's envelope. This is demeaning. It is best for the church to have a wedding policy, complete with fees, fully in place.

Chapter Six

What the Pastor's Spouse Requires

The underlying assumption of this book is that new clergy, no matter how well-trained, do not come to churches ready-made. They need time to develop and grow into what will be their own pastoral identity and style. All this takes time marked by much trial and error. In this chapter we make the same assumption with reference to the new pastor's spouse.

The subject of clergy spouses brings us to one of the key areas in which the contemporary church is quite unlike that of a generation earlier. Consider, for example, that book with which our last chapter started: Carolyn P. Blackwood's *The Pastor's Wife.* This book was published in 1951 and is so extremely dated today that it can hardly serve as a field guide. The title alone is sufficient to show how church life has changed over the last fifty years. In 1951, that title would have gathered in the majority of clergy spouses; today, with an increasing number of women being called to ordained ministry, there is the welcome addition of a number of males to the ranks of clergy spouses. The minister's wife still exists, to be sure, but she is joined in growing numbers by the minister's husband.

We can also note the presence of gay and lesbian clergy. What about their partners? This is a significant question in today's church, a question hardly imagined in yesterday's congregation. For better or worse, I am going to dodge it completely. Please do not take this to mean I am opposed to gay and lesbian clergy. The reason for their omission here is that I believe they and their partners face unique and demanding challenges the dynamics of which call for separate and extensive treatment from someone far more expert. That will need to be another book written by one more qualified.

Most every page of Mrs. Blackwood's work reveals features as dated as her title. The pastor's wife she envisioned did not work outside the home, and, with reference to the church, worked chiefly among the congregation's women and girls. She was homemaker, hostess, occasional Bible study leader, and committee chair or recruiter. She was the answerer of the telephone and the doorbell while her husband was secluded in his study. She was ready with advice, when asked, but was slow to offer her opinions. She helped her husband learn the names of church members and she gently critiqued his sermons, but never on Sunday afternoon. She rarely made calls with her husband, whether in hospitals or homes, but she was an unofficial counselor and woman of prayer. Mrs. Blackwood rather assumed that, even though there were variances from person to person, this described the minister's wife all across Christ's church, or at least across mainline Protestantism.

Today is different. Male spouses are not expected to do this kind of work. Our culture has never assumed the husband would not work outside the home and be little more than an adjunct to his wife's work. That being the case, the men among the spouses are not up against the same pressures as the women.

At the same time, female spouses are little expected today to fit the mold Mrs. Blackwood described fifty years ago. It seems to me that congregations now understand that a minister's wife, like so many other women of the church, will be employed outside the home. The days may not be fully gone, but they are passing, when the pastor's wife was expected to be something of an unofficial and unpaid Associate Pastor.

Nevertheless, no matter how dated the bulk of *The Pastor's Wife* may be, something from Mrs. Blackwood's book still prevails. What prevails is that - rightly or wrongly, fairly or unfairly - the minister's spouse is looked upon by every eye in the congregation and with a different eye. Much has changed in fifty years, but we still live in a time when the pastor and pastor's spouse are public people. It may be inappropriate to call this "celebrity status" but, whatever it is, churches cannot help convey it. It goes with the territory, as it were, and sets ordained ministry apart from medicine, teaching, plumbing, and nearly every other field, with the possible exception of politics. The smaller the town around the church, the more exposed the minister and his or her family are to public view.

Spouses of clergy new to ministry will find themselves thrust into this public position almost without warning and certainly without formal training for it. This gives the first church a profound opportunity perhaps even more significant than that it has with the new pastor. The pastor has had at least three years of seminary training in preparation for his or her calling. You - the first church - may be the first place this pastor's spouse learns anything about his or her newly appointed public role.

A Person Under Pressure

The best way for you to begin to help is to understand that your new pastor's spouse is a person under pressure. Most of this pressure gathers around the theme of role expectations, but there are other pressures as well, such as marital stress and the internal pressure that comes from the desire to see the spouse succeed. A few words about each of these pressures are in order.

Whenever a minister changes churches and starts working someplace new, he or she feels a subtle pressure from the congregation when parishioners speak of the predecessor, whether kindly or unkindly. It may not be the intent of the parishioners to impose this pressure, but it is felt nonetheless. There comes a time in every pastorate when the new minister begins to wince at the mention of Rev. Predecessor's name, for, correctly or incorrectly, Rev. Newcomer hears the old name as an expression of hope or fear that former conditions will be repeated.

Spouses find themselves under the same burden of comparison. As the new spouse is told of what the old spouse did or did not do in and around the church, pressure begins to mount. This is especially true if the former and current spouse are of the same sex. Everything from which friends the former spouse had to where the former sat in the sanctuary will be the topic for discussion. This discussion will not always be with the current mate, but, as we all know, word gets around. Indeed, the intent of these conversations may not be to lay down any law or exert any pressure. Nevertheless, the newcomer feels the shadow of the predecessor everywhere - even at home, if the house is a parsonage. Phrased another way, the new spouse feels under scrutiny early on, always eyed for any signs of being like the previous spouse.

Marital stress complicates these feelings. To raise this issue is not to call the new pastor's marriage into question. I am simply noting that, when ministry begins, there are a number of changes happening in this couple's life all at once, and each one is an inducer of stress which cannot help but be felt by the marriage. The stress of a move, of a new job, and particularly a new career all are capable of putting a heavy strain on the best of marriages. Your new pastor and his or her spouse are facing these in addition to learning about you and about ministry itself. If they seem frazzled and on edge, they deserve the benefit of the doubt.

All this is amplified when ministry is the new pastor's second career, which seems to be more the norm today than it was generations ago. Old ways of relating to one another, forged over time and in relation to one occupation, need reappraisal, adjustment, adaptation, and more in light of the newness of ministry with its new stresses, new demands upon time, and what it does to family life. Ministry is not like other occupations. Clergy do not work their shift and then have their evenings and weekends free. If the new pastor's former occupation allowed that kind of schedule, ministry will at first feel like an intrusion into the marriage. Old patterns will need to be reworked into new forms.

Financial strain can certainly contribute to marital stress. Consider how it is for those new to ministry. Those who entered seminary following a more lucrative career than parish ministry are coming to terms with monthly or biweekly paychecks significantly smaller than they used to be. They are also discovering how the newly acquired seminary degree came prepackaged with loans to repay, and they are finding it increasingly difficult to maintain a balance in their checking account, much less keep a savings account. Meanwhile, opportunities to sink into even deeper debt loiter perilously near. The couple may be handling this financial strain well, but that does not mean it is not felt.

Marital stress of a more serious nature can be lingering in the background as ministry begins in earnest if the pastor's companion is cool to the idea of ministry in the first place. Here there are any number of "what ifs" we could suppose, but not finally answer because we ourselves are not in the marriages we are reflecting upon. But what if a spouse agreed to the whole seminary thing thinking the call to ministry was more a whim his or her partner was having than the voice of God? What if this spouse went along with seminary hoping all the while seminary would help the other "get over" the crazy compulsion to be a pastor? If seminary did not change the person's mind, ordination and the call to a particular church is his or her spouse's worst case scenario, even if the first church is of the highest caliber. Any pressure the congregation puts on this spouse to be anything in the church may be like detonating a fuse or winding the clock on a time-bomb.

The spouse who wants his or her partner to be a pastor and is 100% supportive of the call to ministry feels pressure of another kind. This is best described as an internal pressure that is the desire to see his or her mate succeed and look good in the eyes of the congregation. The husband of a clergywoman reported to me that he is aware of cultural undertones which still believe female clergy are less capable than their male counterparts and that women are less capable than men in general in positions of leadership. He deliberately backs off from heavy involvement in the church so his newly ordained wife will be seen independently of him and capable in her own right.

While this man does little so his wife will look good, my wife has always sought to do much so I will look good. Without compromising her own interests or abilities, and without pushing herself into church activities already run by others, she has, over all our years together, found ways to be active toward the good of the church. She does this out of Christian conviction, to be sure, but also out of marital love. She knows I will be happier with the church, and the church will be happier with me, if things are going well. Her gift, to me and the church, has been to look for areas that are weak and, if able, do all she can to make them strong.

Thus there are at least two ways of responding to the same internal pressure. The clergywoman's husband and my wife want the pastors in their lives to look good in the eyes of their congregations. Both find what is the right course of action for them. What makes this a form of pressure is that the spouses have an eye on the congregation in a vigilant attempt to gauge the congregation's response. Outwardly these spouses may not appear to be ill at ease or under duress, but they do not have inner calm either. An unvoiced question is always nagging them, as it is their spouses: How are things going with the church?

A Person in Their Own Right

We have been thinking so far about pressures the new clergy's spouse is under. It is important for the church to recognize that the congregation cannot keep spouses from feeling these pressures. No matter how fine the congregation is, ministry in the church will carry with it various strains, tensions and duresses that will be felt both by pastors and their marriage partners. While the congregation cannot prevent pastors and spouses from feeling these burdens, they can work to refrain from adding to them. The best way to do this is to see the spouse as a person in his or her own right, and loving them for who they are.

The place to begin this understanding and love is with the spouse's name. The theme song for *Cheers*, a popular television series from a few years back, sang that people want to go where everyone knows their name. Clergy spouses want to go where people know and use their names. They want their own identity to stand out. When I asked a number of them what I should be writing in this chapter, this was a near unanimous response. One said she liked to be introduced to others by name and not as "my pastor's wife." Another testified to being filled with joy when a church member introduced her to someone else by saying, "This is my friend Jody." When their preferred or given name is used, spouses feel respected and appreciated, less tied to a preconceived role and less darkened by a predecessor's shadow.

It is critically important for the congregation to recognize the pastor's spouse is a person with distinct gifts and interests. They are glad to bring these to the church and legitimately miffed when the congregation expects them to be something else altogether simply because of the one to whom they are married. Congregations can release the pressure of role expectations by refusing to impose a double-standard which is so often applied. The new pastor's spouse, typically but not necessarily, is a new member of the church. Is more expected of this new member than of others because their spouse is the pastor? The moment this new member is expected to do more than other new members and to assume a specific role is the moment an unfair double-standard is put into place. It is absolutely important for congregations to recognize their pastor's husband or wife is an individual with distinct gifts and interests. Everyone will benefit when the congregation lets them choose when, how, and to what extent they will be active in the life of the church.

The wife of a clergyman who started in ministry in Iowa thirty years ago tells of a day not long after they took up residence in the parsonage. The doorbell rang and, when she went to answer it, the minister's wife found a parishioner standing there holding a typewriter. Handing the typewriter to the dumbfounded spouse, the parishioner said, "The church has a new minister. The new minister has a wife, so the church has a new secretary!" Others in that same church were puzzled and upset the new minister's wife did not teach piano lessons. We who have never been party to these kinds of experiences can find them comical, but they are devastating to those who find themselves expected to live under these conditions and in a preconceived role.

One spouse who has been burned in these ways in the past now prefers to be left out of the formal interviews when a search committee meets with her husband. This helps everyone understand that she is not applying for any job and will not be the one hired in any case. There is perhaps some wisdom in her practice. If the search committee would like to come to know the candidate's spouse, that can take place more socially, over meals and informal conversations. Let the formal interview be with the candidate alone, for the candidate alone will be the one hired. Spouses are not adjunct or Associate Pastors. Married clergy are not a "two-for-one" deal for the church.

Of course, as indicated earlier, most spouses are eager to be part of the church and contribute what they can along the lines of their own interests, abilities and availabilities. No formal rules can be applied. Individuals are unique and each marriage structures itself differently. One minister's spouse whom I know has accepted positions on committees and boards of the church all throughout the long years of her husband's ministry. Another has refused to do that on the assumption it may put the clergyperson in an awkward position or lead parishioners to suppose the minister's partner is after power. Some have been Sunday School teachers, and others members of the choir. Some have assumed neither of those roles but have found other ways to be active. Again, it all depends upon the individual and what his or her gifts and interests may be. The role is never rightly defined by others or ahead of time.

It can be noted briefly that this refers to the spouse's life outside the church as well as within the congregation. At one point in our marriage, my wife thought about obtaining a real estate license but demurred, not knowing how people in the community would take to the idea of a minister's wife showing houses. The church we were in at the time knew nothing of her thinking and did nothing to discourage her. I raise this now only to point out that spouses themselves can feel a bit constrained by what the church might think when it comes to what occupation they pursue. These feelings might increase if the matter were not an occupation but a public office, like village trustee or school board member. Should the pastor's spouse be allowed to occupy positions such as these? If the partners of the marriage agree, the church has nothing to say. It should be a general rule that the church not limit the spouse's life or expression of individuality.

As a person in his or her own right, the minister's spouse is someone in need of friendships. Earlier chapters have stressed the difficulties for clergy in being friends with persons inside the church. Much the same applies to the spouse. Ministry is as lonely for the spouse as it is for the pastor. Church life puts us around church people more than any others, but these are the very ones with whom we cannot develop close friendships. We can have loving *pastoral* relationships, to be sure, but this is something different from genuine friendship, which simply cannot happen with church members.

This seems cruel and hard for parishioners to understand, so it merits emphasizing once more. Clergy and their spouses cannot have close personal friendships with church members for a number of key reasons. A counseling situation may develop and, if the pastor has cultivated friendship with the parishioner, all objectivity may be lost, and this can imperil the pastor's ability to be of true help. If the church member serves on a board or a committee, a difference of opinion may develop between this and other members of the group, and this imperils the minister's ability to be a pastor to all and see the group through any conflict which may ensue. More significantly and more pointedly in terms of the spouse, allegations of favoritism can undermine ministerial effectiveness and congregational morale in a very short order. All this means you who are church members can count on your minister and his or her spouse to like you a lot, but some boundary line will be drawn of necessity. This will be for your sake, the church's, and that of Mr. and Mrs. Minister.

Though it is unadvisable for the spouse to have very good friends in the church, it is ideal for them to have extremely good allies in the church. Boundaries will exist, to be sure, but these allies will feel like friends to a certain degree. These will be people who understand it isn't always easy to be married to the one the congregation looks up to. They will understand it isn't always easy to be one who is under the scrutiny of the congregation or the shadow of one's predecessor. They will be people who take the new pastor's spouse under their wing, as it were, and help them understand that no one in the congregation takes the Busybody family seriously or listens to the complaints of the Whines, who have aggravated ministers for decades. These allies set picks and dish out grains of salt. They love the spouse unconditionally and do what they can to help them find the personal space to be themselves.

A Person with Confidences to Honor

An area that deserves special mention is that of the keeping of secrets. Ministry depends upon the keeping of confidences. Ministry simply cannot happen without a sure and profound trust between pastor and parishioner. Parishioners have to be able to rely upon the minister's ability to honor their trust when they share with them matters they want the minister to keep in strict confidence. This is essential to an effective pastorate.

Spouses honor these confidences. Speaking personally, I am happy to report Sherrol asks no questions. Oh, of course, when I return from a hospital call, she may ask how I found so-and-so, but, if I announce to her that I have a meeting with a couple or a person at my church office, she does not ask who it is or what it is about. She knows the importance honoring confidences has to ministry, and she knows the value trust has to marriage. We trust each other implicitly. She knows nothing will happen illicitly. She respects me and the parishioners enough to not pry into what is rightly confidential.

Congregations need to honor these confidences, too. Parishioners should ask no prying questions of the spouse, hoping to get the low-down on a third party's condition, complaint, crisis, or conduct. Questions by the overly curious are invitations to betrayal, and they put the spouse in a position that is only awkward and uncomfortable. The truest allies will never ask such questions, and they will tell others they should not ask them either.

A Person with a Family

One of the best gifts a congregation can give a pastor's spouse is the understanding that he or she is a person with a family that needs time to be together and away from the church. Ministry can take all the pastor's time if we let it, and it is the temptation of pastors and churches to let it occupy a great deal of time, often at the expense of the pastor's family. The spouse will receive it as a gift when the congregation encourages the pastor to take a day off and then honors that time off by not making any demands or encroachments on that near sacred day. The spouse will receive it as an even greater gift when the congregation keeps the minister's hours to a reasonable limit and does not eat up every evening with meetings or other gatherings.

This allows for the support of the pastor's children as well as the pastor's spouse. Concerts, Little League games, soccer games, piano recitals - these are important activities in the life of children, and no church should ask a pastor to miss them save in the most unavoidable of circumstances. Only a real emergency should keep the minister away. When the pastor is expected to miss this or that meeting for the sake of his or her children, the kids feel blessed and the spouse does not feel like a single parent. Every church has it within its means to grant pastors, spouses and pastor's children this gift.

Both the pastor and his or her companion will respond well when the church places no burdens on the children of the parsonage. I am proud to say that our children - now nearly grown - all rather enjoy being "PKs" - preacher's kids. This is a gift from God Most High, to be sure, but a gift given through the churches of which we have been a part. At the first church I served, our three, the first little children in the parsonage in some thirty years, were welcomed into the church like grandchildren. The members of the congregation nearly spoiled them with positive attention and love unashamed and unreserved. They were received in much the same way when we arrived at my second church, even though they were a little older. Here they have been given positive support, support which has been clear but not overbearing. Church members, again like grandparents, have attended their concerts and ball games, remembered their birthdays and noted their presence on the school's honor roll. Above all, they have known them by name and loved them for the individuals they are.

This brings us back full circle to the surest advice any church can be given about how to respond to a new pastor's spouse. The key is to receive each individual as an individual, and to come to know and love them for the people they are. Learn and use their names, let them be themselves, and help them find their own way. In time, the chances are the church will discover the new spouse to be a blessing to be cherished.

Chapter Seven

What the Second Year Brings

Unless they are Ralph and Alice Kramden, honeymooners are happy, glowing, and full of the brightness of the future. Their days are ideal, almost carefree, as they begin to make their way in life together. But, like all good things, honeymoons come to an end. To be sure, this does not mean the marriage is in trouble. On the contrary, the end of the honeymoon means the marriage is maturing. It is simply, though perhaps ingloriously, moving into a new dimension, one deeper and more developed than the first.

It is common to speak of a minister's first year or so with a congregation as the honeymoon period. The phrase is apt, for the early months of a pastorate are full of an odd mixture of excitement, discovery, nervousness, and naivety, all of which are honeymoon-like. These days come to an end as well. Here we are thinking they begin to end sometime during the second year. Seminaries, because they "empty into" the first year, tend to do a good job preparing students for ministry's beginning months, but they give little thought to the ensuing years, especially the second, which can be far more difficult than the first. Managing the second year and its difficulties calls upon the pastor's ability to think, make adjustments, and continue his or her preparation for ministry. It also calls upon the church's ability to weather change, adapt to new circumstances, and voice opinions constructively with gentleness and integrity.

Since making the transition from honeymoon to mature relationship depends as much upon the congregation as it does upon the pastor, the second year merits our special consideration. What makes the second year more difficult than the first? Two developments: volunteers step back and critics step up.

Volunteers Step Back

After the initial shock of a minister's resignation and the closure brought about by that minister's departure, a congregation's attention shifts from the pastor to the pastoral office. The focus moves from a person newly gone to a series of tasks needing to be done. The sense of an indefinite "in the meantime" begins to grow among the people as they realize church life will be different until a new pastor comes upon the scene. They may have an interim minister in place, but, in most cases, this is a part-time position, and the interim cannot be expected to do the same amount of work the former resident pastor did. If that work is to be accomplished, it needs to be accomplished by volunteers from the congregation.

This is an invigorating time for congregations as, one by one, people step up to help carry on the work of the church. Given the length of time the average search takes, an entire cycle of the church year can be conducted in this manner. Whether they are the chairs of various boards or committees or volunteers who have taken on particular tasks, those who step up during the interim period carry the load of responsibility. They function as true leaders. They may look to the part-time interim for guidance, but they do not lean on the interim in quite the same way as they would a resident. They develop a kind of pride of ownership in the administrative and programmatic work of the church, and feel a distinct sense of satisfaction when the wheels of the church's machinery keep humming.

A good deal of this increased volunteer activity continues into the first year of the new minister's watch. The pride of ownership they have developed, and the fact that they, not the new pastor, are the ones "in the know" about the church's schedule and functions, keep them highly charged and actively involved. They remember both the work and the fun of gearing up for a particular season of the church year, and they are excited to be part of it again, if only to relive that former joy. The new pastor is thrilled, of course, by this amount of energy and productivity coming from the lay leaders of the church. The new congregation is an exciting place to be.

By the second year, however, the folks who carried the ball during the interim period and who took the lead during the beginning months of the new pastorate, are ready to take some time off. Some version of the Parable of the Sower applies here, for the volunteers draw back from their positions of responsibility for a variety of reasons. A few, it is safe to say, simply lose interest. They were excited for a while, but when the excitement of searching for a new minister subsided, so did their excitement over being actively involved in as church workers. Others draw back because they lose their sense of urgency once the crisis of a vacant pulpit has passed and the presence of pastoral staff means the church's program is no longer in jeopardy. Another handful may step back because they accomplished what they set out to do. They helped the church through a difficult time but are now ready to return to their former, though less prominent, position in the church. While they could find the time to fulfill a larger role for a brief year or two, their life situation is such that they cannot maintain this level of activity over a longer course.

Significant numbers, however, alter their place and level of activity in the congregation because the church's constitution requires it. The second year of a pastorate witnesses the minister's first experience with the natural change of officers as mandated by the church's structure. While it may be beneficial to have removed from positions of power certain persons who were there during the previous pastor's stay, this change in congregational leadership is a critical moment in the life of the new ministry. The persons whose terms expire during the second year of a pastorate are the ones with whom the new pastor was just beginning to develop rapport and a working relationship complete with trust. Those who will take their place may occupy that position for up to as many as six years if they accept a second term. It is very possible, of course, that these new leaders could be as capable as - or more capable that - the outgoing ones, but there is initial nervousness in the pastor's heart because the new slate of officers is not as well known as the older crew.

All this means the second year makes for a kind of starting over. The momentum that was generated by the thrill of seeking a new pastor and by riding out the interim period peters out sometime during this second year as some volunteers tire and others are cycled out of their roles. A new momentum needs to be generated. Without it, the downward pull of a dying momentum drags the church into a dispirited mood. The new pastor cannot help the fact that yesterday's momentum slows. That is part of the natural course of a church's life. But the responsibility of generating a new momentum falls, under God, largely upon the pastor's shoulders. It tests the new pastor's ability to lead. This testing makes the second year more challenging than the first.

Lay people can help their new pastor at this critical time by paying the utmost of attention to the nominating process. The responsibility for generating new momentum may fall largely upon the new pastor's shoulders but it never falls wholly upon the pastor. Every church needs the right kind of lay leadership at this moment. Nominating committees should be in place and they should be after people who will both say "yes" and do a good job. Warm bodies who do nothing but hold down a chair are not what is needed when the second year of a pastorate tries to work against the dying momentum of the first year's enthusiasm. In subsequent years, the minister will be able to provide the nominating committee with a great deal of assistance because, by that time, he or she will be very well acquainted with the gifts and abilities of most everyone in the church. But the pastor is not in this position in the second year. Lay people still know the other lay people better, and they need to work to find church officers who will be assets to the ongoing life of the congregation.

This is experience writing. The church I currently serve not only started to lose momentum in its Christian Education department beginning my second year, a negative momentum began to grow. Much of this was my fault because I recruited the wrong person for an important post. The Sunday School Superintendent who had done a fantastic job during the interim period and my first year resigned because she and her husband were moving to a different state. Concurrent to this, the leadership on our Board of Christian Education was undergoing a near complete transition as well. Two of its more gifted members were departing because their terms were coming to an end. Staying on the Board was a woman who was placed on the Board, I later discovered, because she was a vocal critic of the Sunday School program. Those who nominated her figured giving her a position of responsibility would have her, frankly, put up or shut up. She did neither, and we had to endure her complaints - now no longer tempered and handled by the departed and more experienced Board members - until her term expired a year later.

Meanwhile, I suggested for Superintendent a man who gave me every appearance of being a pillar in the church. He and his family were in worship nearly every Sunday. They missed perhaps only one or two worship services a year. He came to the Bible studies I offered early on, and his comments and questions led me to believe he was "with it" in terms of knowledge of the Bible and of Christian doctrine. I could tell that he even read a little theology of a serious nature and not just the fluff that passes for theological material. All this made him seem to me to be an ideal candidate for the position of Sunday School Superintendent, and the Board of Christian Education went along with that recommendation. The man agreed to the post without hesitation.

What I thought was a success turned out to be disaster. I do not wish to be perceived as speaking negatively about this man, for his heart was in the right place. I still think him to be a good man. He may even have been a good Sunday School Superintendent. But not for this church. He had a theological agenda that diverged not only from mine but from that of the congregation in particular and our denomination as a whole. To his credit, he was dedicated to his task and faithful to his mission; to my dismay, his task and mission were not ones the congregation supported. We were in this predicament for some time before matters were resolved. I report, with sadness and regret, that there were some ugly meetings and sharp exchanges as the situation came to a head.

My point is not to relive an old battle on these pages but to show how disaster can be averted by a hard-working nomination process that takes its task seriously. I was late to realize that numbers of the core members of the church, that is, persons who had been part of the congregation for long years, were little surprised that trouble developed. Our new Superintendent was liked by members of the congregation but he was also known to have distinctive ideas. Had that been known by me ahead of time, the recommendation that he be appointed would never have been made. This may have kept him and his family in our fellowship. It certainly would have prevented us from losing such momentum in the Sunday School that we nearly crashed and burned.

The moral of the story is, help your church and your new pastor find the right kind of leaders for the crucial second year when so many seeds will be sown for subsequent years.

Critics Rise Up

Critics of the pastor begin to rise up during the second year. Some of these are the habitually critical. Every church and organization has them. They are "contrarians" who do not seem to be happy unless they are against something, even if it is to say the church's water is too wet. They may keep quiet during the new minister's first year as they size up the new situation, but they are gathering material nonetheless. The changes that start occurring the second year - or those that do not take place - can start them humming.

New critics are a more serious threat than the habitually critical. Most congregations know how to deflect the remarks of chronic complainers, but new voices of criticism, especially if they were former voices of support within the church, are much more difficult to manage. These voices begin to speak up the second year. This is because the newness of the new pastorate does not really begin until the second year. The new minister's first year, or at least much of it, is mostly reconnaissance as he or she surveys the field of the new parish, learning the life and structure of the local congregation, and deciding what needs to be done. Sometime during the second year, new programs are introduced and new policies are proposed. These begin to put the stamp of the new pastor's personality, theology, gifts and visions on the work of the church. Instead of teaching new duties, the new occasions brought about by new programs and proposals bring new opportunities to complain. Up to now, the new minister had been going along with things pretty much as they were; now changes are taking place and resistance always accompanies change.

The most difficult critic with which to contend is one who was presumed to be an ally. As the second year progresses, allies are tested and not all remain the allies the pastor thought they might be. When my present congregation voted on me to become its pastor, the vote was not unanimous. Eleven voted against me. I did not take these as votes against me as much as I did as votes for the other person whom I was aware some in the congregation wanted. The interim who preceded me was very thoughtful and up front with me in saying there was a cadre of people fairly insistent that he be called as resident pastor. The Association Minister and the Search Committee told me the same thing. I knew the names of some who were in this cadre, particularly the leaders of it, but not of all. At any rate, just days after we moved into our new home, one of those whom I took to be a leader of this group, brought a cake to our house as a gift of welcome. This person and I later worked on a project she had already successfully begun under the interim; I encouraged its continuation and supported the project wholeheartedly. Everything was going well, so I thought a would-be critic was developing into an ally. But she and her husband were gone in a year.

The advent of criticism and the departure of parishioners cause pastoral hearts to ache, for they bring to an undistinguished end relationships that showed early promise. This ache is acute enough in seasoned pastors, but they have the benefit of experience which tells them they shall get beyond it and their pastorate shall survive and maybe even thrive. Second year clergy do not have the benefit of this seasoning, so the first conflicts and first losses can be devastating to morale and to hope.

Perhaps it is not inappropriate to compare this to professional baseball players. All hitters run into slumps where their batting average takes a nosedive. For whatever reasons, they stop getting the hits they are accustomed to getting. They strike out. They pop up. They ground out. They do not get the ball out of the infield. Along the way, they leave men on base and do not help their team win. Veteran hitters have been in those situations before and have come out of them. Hitting a slump aggravates them, to be sure, for they want to do well, but they have the confidence of knowing they will hit again. They have gotten out of slumps before and they will once more. Rookie batters do not have the benefit of this experience. Their first slump may lead them to believe that they cannot hit major league pitching after all. Veteran players and coaches work to help the rookie psychologically as well as mechanically during these periods so that the first slump does not lead to the defeat of an otherwise good player.

In the ministry, every pastor worthy of the title grieves the loss of parishioners when members leave a church because of some disagreement or disappointment. These losses may mark some kind of victory for the pastor's proposals or perspectives, but they are losses to the congregation nonetheless, and they are mourned by the ministers who feel responsible for them. Moreover, even veteran clergy fear their pastorates may not be able to survive many "victories" like this. But they are buoyed in their grief and fear by the experience of having survived such losses before and from having seen how the process of working through criticism can make the church stronger. New ministers do not have this kind of history to draw upon. Their first critics and their first losses loom much larger and threaten to undo everything. Unless the pastor has some way of processing this grief and fear, his or her spirit can become raw.

In time, a Pastoral Relations Committee will be able to benefit the minister who is facing criticism, but in the early years of a pastorate, even for a veteran minister, Pastoral Relations Committees are almost impossible to develop, at least to the level at which they can be helpful. Effective Pastoral Relations Committees are composed of persons trusted and chosen by the pastor, respected and honored by members of the congregation, and appointed by the Church Council or other governing board. They are sounding boards for ideas, channels of communication to whom persons of the congregation can go when complaints arise, and confidants with whom the pastor can unburden himself or herself in an atmosphere of confidentiality. It is next to impossible to know, by the second year of a pastorate, which persons can and should be trusted with this highly sensitive position in the church.

The strategy of using the Search Committee as the initial Pastoral Relations Committee can be called into question. This strategy shows a degree of promise, to be sure, for the members of the Search Committee are the first persons whom the pastor comes to know rather well, and these are the first in the church who have the opportunity to know the pastor and, particularly, the pastor's way of thinking and working. Nevertheless, the tasks of the two bodies are distinct and call for different skills. Qualities that make a person a good Search Committeeman may not make for a good member of a Pastoral Relations Committee.

Besides, it is difficult to keep active and together a committee that feels it has done its job. The members of the hard-working Search Committee may be the first who are ready for a long rest after the new pastor arrives on the scene. Even if they have energy left, if a controversy develops, they may not be perceived by the other members of the congregation as impartial or above the fray. It could be that they would be automatically perceived as being on the pastor's side, since they were his or her first advocates, and this may stifle any sane conversation that could dismantle a difficulty or disarm a controversy.

Further, it is worth noting that the church in its second year of a new pastorate is always different from the church it was at the time of the former minister's departure. The conditions which made the persons on the Search Committee representative of the congregation as a whole may no longer prevail into the new minister's term. This is especially true if the Search Committee was not carefully chosen in the first place.

Thus, one of the chief difficulties facing a second year pastor is that of not knowing whom to trust or where to turn when voices of criticism begin to be heard and members of the church start to walk. What can the congregation do to help at this critical stage? When the couple who wanted the interim pastor to stay left, my biggest help came from those who expressed to me words of support for me and my ministry. The best of these words came from another couple who were part of the cadre that wanted the interim. I would not have known that had they not told me. By telling me they were in my corner after having been in the other camp, by saying they did not understand why the other couple left, and by reassuring me I should not take that departure personally, they made me stronger. They did not draw any public battle lines, but they did not keep their feelings of support for me a secret from me. They spoke up, and that was a strength.

Along with supporting the pastor where that is advisable, congregations should encourage healthy criticism of and within the church. Members who criticize ministers are not necessarily in the wrong. Even chronic complainers can have legitimate beefs. Right critiques need to be expressed for the good of the congregation and the growth of the ministry just beginning. But there are wrong ways to voice right complaints. Every parishioner who gets an ear-full from another, whether it is about the minister or some other aspect of the church's life, should direct that person to voice their concerns to the proper body. Instead of getting sucked into an issue, it is better to say something like, "If that is the way you feel, then you should talk to the pastor or share your concerns with the Council." The more this kind of thing happens, the more effectively genuine complaints will be addressed and the less damaging petty complaining will be.

A wonderful thing congregations can do is simply keep calm. Those who stay calm help keep others from over-reacting. Volunteers may be stepping back and critics may be stepping up, but all this can be more a return to normalcy than a rising crisis. The honeymoon period of the pastorate may be coming to a close, but the pastorate itself is not falling apart. The luster that once was is simply fading. I refer to the luster the congregation tried to write into its congregational profile and the luster the pastor tried to write into his or her professional profile. Both parties are, by the second year of their relationship, discovering that the other hid a wart or two. This exposure is not necessarily pleasant, but, by the same token, it is not necessarily reason for panic, either. It is more a time for accepting one another, warts and all, and learning to love the idiosyncracies that make the other unique. Only those who are calm and who help a spirit of calm prevail can move a congregation and its pastor toward this maturity. If pastor and congregation can embrace one another during this awkward period that is the second year, give or take a few months, then the future looks bright.

Chapter Eight

What the Joys of the Pastorate Can Be

The Christian Century recently reported on the present shortage of young pastors in the mainline denominations (Vol. 118, No. 12, April 11, 2001, p. 16-23). A veteran pastor responded in a subsequent issue (Vol. 118, No. 16, May 16, 2001, p. 28) with an anonymous letter to the editor. Sadly, this person's letter concentrates on the detriments of pastoral ministry and blames the shortage of young pastors on the church for its habit of making ministerial lives miserable. Why encourage a young person to enter a field full of woe?

My own view is that pastoral ministry, though full of difficulty, is rich with rewards unparalleled in any other vocation. My perspective throughout these pages has been that the minister's first church has a unique opportunity to help an inexperienced pastor work through the difficulties associated with our calling and come to enjoy its unique privileges. If this can be done successfully, then chances of the innocent rookie becoming an embittered veteran significantly decrease. As that chance decreases, the chances increase that this person now in love with ministry will stay in it and inspire others toward it. For a church to be instrumental in this is to enhance the kingdom of God.

We have spent considerable time considering the difficulties of ministry and how churches can help pastors contend with them. Now it is time to name the joys of pastoral ministry and indicate in some measure how first churches can nurture them into experience. The best I can do here is name my chief satisfactions and call upon individual congregations to so come to know their pastors that they learn what makes them tick and what brings them joy.

Being with People at Significant Moments

Moments after one of the pillars of the church died in his home, his wife telephoned me with the news. I was able to be with this couple in their home before the funeral directors arrived to take the man's body away. Their daughter was there, too, and two hospice nurses arrived shortly after I did. Scenes such as this are sacred, loving, awesomely personal. To be invited into them is to be invited into the most important moments of a person's life.

There are some days that are filled with this kind of emotional intensity when you are a pastor. The day before writing the words you are reading now, I was with the family of an elderly man who died, with a young couple expecting their first child and wanting the join the church, and I heard the broken voice of a mother telling me through tears of her teen-aged son's attempted suicide. Days such as this are exhausting, to be sure, but there is a certain spiritual reward that accompanies them. The reward comes with the realization that it is a privilege to be allowed to be present at these significant times in the lives of individuals and families.

Not every thrilling moment in ministry is a life-threatening one. There are any number of them scattered across the years of my ministry. I think of the Confirmand who sat in my study and said he wanted to do more to serve the church. I think of the woman with time on her hands who called to ask if there was someone she could visit. I think of the woman who, with a year full of blessings in her life, sent a generous but anonymous gift to the church as a thank offering.

The people experiencing these moments, both the dramatic and the undramatic, were on life's frontier. They were at the border of an experience and an existence wholly new to them and fully untried from their perspective. It is quite beside the point to say others have known moments like these before because the more important fact is that *these* people had never faced *this* before. The children of the elderly man who died had never seen the world before without their Dad in it. The couple expecting a child have not known a world with their son or daughter in it. The mother whose son attempted suicide had hitherto no idea what it was like to be the Mom of a boy so desperate as to want to die. These people were at the edge, at the border where one kind of life becomes another.

These frontiers are the places of God's gracious activity today. The God in whom we believe is not an Idea we can recall but a Person who draws near, keeping the promise to be present with us all along the twists and turns of the pilgrimage of life. Our faith is that God is at work at these frontiers, bringing resurrection and calling abundant living into being. As such, the frontier is the place of God's mission of comfort, reconciliation, recreation, and revelation.

Pastoral ministry takes place on these frontiers. We are invited to them in a way few others are. Celebrating a birth, attending a death, fighting a sickness, admitting the burden of a heavy strain - this is the stuff of life, and most people handle it personally and privately. Few get to glimpse more than a public face. But clergy are allowed into the intimacy of what people are like when they face something alone. Clergy do not see people in the nude the way physicians do, but we are almost constantly in the presence of naked souls. All of this involves a holiness and a sanctity only an oaf would take lightly.

Sensitive pastors know they are present at these life-defining moments not in their own right or upon their own behalf. They are present instead as ambassadors of the kingdom, as representatives of Jesus Christ and the love of God.

To be present as a nervous and piddling human being, yet as one whom God is using in ways unexplained, is something that never ceases to both amaze and humble.

One of the important functions the parishioners of a pastor's first church can perform is to allow their pastor entrance into their own lives at moments such as these. The new minister's inexperience may cause folks to hesitate in the thought that one new to the work may not know what to say or do. The fact is that the veteran probably does not know, either. But God is hard at work in the silences of the awkward moments and in the gaps between our broken words. As God so ministers to, through, and in spite of us, the hearts of pastor and people grow closer together, the church is strengthened, a minister is made, and new life begins to spring forth.

Having Opportunities to be of Influence

In addition to being present with people at the significant moments in their lives, one of the joys of ministry is found in having opportunities to be of influence. Stating it thus can make it seem as though joy is found in being a person of power. That is not my meaning. I refer here more to the surprise of effectiveness than to any exercise of power. Whatever power and ability are displayed through us come from God who makes ministry effective. We humans are but earthen vessels in the divine work. Our joy stems from learning we have been used by God to effect something good.

We have opportunities to be influential in the lives of individual persons. Our work is such that it seldom shows immediate results. In this it is quite unlike mowing the lawn or shoveling snow. We have few times when we can look back and actually see that we accomplished anything. But when we are given the vision of something that was accomplished because of our efforts, however humble, there is great rejoicing in the pastoral heart. A minister's face was beaming when she told of what happened because of a Lenten sermon series she preached. The series was on forgiveness, both its difficulties and its possibilities. She was told that one of the sermons in the series so moved a couple in her congregation that they sought out reconciliation with some former very good friends of theirs with whom they had a falling out three years earlier. Nothing on earth was broader than the pastor's smile as she told this story. The glint in her eye revealed tears of joy, which in turn revealed a grateful heart newly empowered for and encouraged in ministry.

Another pastor tells of returning to a former place of ministry where the church he once served was celebrating an anniversary. A young man, whom the minister remembered and recognized but could not name, came up to him during the social hour. The pastor half-expected nothing more than a cordial and polite greeting, and, especially since he could not put a name to the face, prepared himself for a warmly formal and slightly awkward exchange. To his great surprise, the fellow said, "If it weren't for you, I don't think I'd be part of the church today, and I just want to say thanks." The pastor was too shocked to ask what it was he had done and he could not find in his memory any indication that he had done anything at all that would have influenced this guy. Apparently the right hand had done something the left hand did not know about, and God was glorified.

In addition to having opportunities to influence individuals, even without our awareness of it, we have the chance to shape congregations. One pastor takes quiet pride in the realization that the church she serves was, during the previous pastor's term, an eyelash or two away from leaving the denomination of which it is a part. The congregation did everything it could to do as little as possible to benefit the wider church. When it contributed money to the work of the denomination, it carefully designated every penny to make sure none of the donation went to promote efforts the congregation thought dubious. During the course of one congregational meeting, the church even voted to send a "statement" to the denomination by contributing only one dollar! Meanwhile, the number of parachurch organizations the congregation supported increased dramatically. All that was more than ten years ago. Now the church participates fully in the activities of the denomination and has redirected its mission dollars away from the parachurch groups and back toward the ministries of its own denomination. Instead of trying to bolt from the denomination this congregation seeks ways to bolster the denomination. This does not mean it is always in agreement with the denomination, but it does mean the church sees itself in lasting partnership with the denomination. The pastor knows she cannot take full credit for this turnaround, but she rightly believes she has had a hand in it by way of the attitude she has taken toward the denomination. When she looks back upon her career and wonders what she has done, she names this to herself as one of her best accomplishments and deepest joys.

Opportunities to influence entire communities also accrue to pastors. The work of John Wesley is often credited with transforming England in the eighteenth century and a sermon by George W. Truett (d. 1945) is remembered as having influenced the Texas Legislature's vote on a bill regarding horse racing. Most of us do not have these large opportunities, but we have real opportunities to impact the towns in which we serve. This can be through our outside involvements or more directly through our work with the church by nature of the programs we support or ministries we help establish.

Parishioners, of course, cannot make their pastors effective, but they can provide feedback to let them know when and how they have been effective. Taking a few moments to write a note or express some word of appreciation in person can do wonders to strengthen a pastor's joy in ministry. After all, everyone likes to hear not only that their efforts were appreciated but that they paid off in some practical way. The more forthright you are with your pastor along these lines, the greater will be your pastor's sense of job satisfaction. This, in turn, will enhance his or her willingness to attempt even more.

Spending Time with Books

Earlier I told of the man who helped me move into my first church. When he was carrying a box of books out of my childhood home and to the truck, he quipped, "I hope you're not planning to read all these books because we want you to do something when you get by us!" It was a line in jest. I did not fully understand that to be the case at the time, but after I came to know that man better I knew he had been teasing. He himself believes reading should be every Christian's responsibility, and he knows reading is an essential part of a minister's work.

The nature of our work is such that we are given the leisure of the study. Here the word *leisure* does not refer to rest but to freedom. In the best of circumstances clergy are freed from other responsibilities so they can spend a concentrated amount of time with books. Parishioners by and large do not have this privilege. Those who read have to work harder than their pastors to carve out the time reading takes. Alert pastors recognize that they have this time given to them if they will but take it.

We ministers need to recall, as do our laypeople, that the reading we do is not alongside of or in addition to our ministry. Reading *is* our ministry. It is our work. We read so we can preach, teach, counsel and pray. We read so that we will be like the scribe Jesus described in Matthew 13.52: "Therefore every scribe trained for the kingdom of heaven is like the master of a household who brings out of his treasure what is new and what is old." Pastors read to become scribes trained for the kingdom, persons who can take what they read and turn it into practical help for the persons under their charge in the economy of God.

Additionally, I have hungered for a reading life as a way of making friends and finding mentors as a pastor. We have already seen how it is a difficult undertaking for clergy to find friends and mentors in ministry. All our other interpersonal relationships make this exceedingly difficult. But friends are near at hand through books. The reading of religious biography in particular has been an absolute boon to my soul on more than one occasion for it has put colleagues and mentors as near as my heart. Following the ups and downs of their pastorates has helped me weather my own and has kept me from feeling utterly alone. For this reason and more, books are sheer joy.

Local churches should do all they can to promote their pastors' reading. Every church can find ways to help the pastor's study be a true study and not simply the church office where the phone rings endlessly and people come and go at will.

They can safeguard the minister's hours for study by hiring a part-time secretary to deal with the telephone, the copy machine, the bulletin, the newsletter, and almost everything else that does not require a seminary degree. Congregations can supply their pastors with a generous book allowance to encourage and make possible the purchase of numerous good books on a variety of pertinent subjects. Perhaps above all, congregations can refuse to speak of the minister's reading as idle time. Parishioners may even encourage reading by asking what the minister has read lately, by suggesting books, and by sharing notes from the books they have read.

Enjoying the Freedom to Structure Time

In ministry, there is time that is not one's own. Our weekends are not free. Many of our weekday evenings are not free, either. Very few of our holidays come without occupational demands, and even our days off can be claimed by legitimate pastoral necessities. We are always on call, and most of us have had our sleep disturbed in the middle of the night by the ringing of the telephone summoning us to some bedside of grief or pain. From this point of view, our lives are scheduled and we have to live out of the calendar constantly.

It is equally true, however, that there is a time we have that others do not. There is time that is not our own, but there is also time that is very much our own and we are free to structure it as we see fit. Some years ago, when our son was in elementary school, I received a telephone call at the church office. It was our son, asking if I could come to school that afternoon for the "Pumpkin Parade" his class was having. Each student had decorated a pumpkin to represent a President of the United States. His was Ulysses S. Grant. All things considered, the "Pumpkin Parade" was not much of anything; the fact that I was there, however, was everything to our son. There were a couple of Moms in the classroom, but I was the only Dad. Getting "off work" that afternoon was no problem for me; it was impossible for others.

My schedule has allowed me to do much over the years that other fathers did not have the opportunity to do, though I am sure they had the will. I could chaperone field trips, drive kids to orthodontia appointments, and be at the school in minutes if a child called sick. I have been able to make it a regular practice to be home when the children come home from school full of the news of their day. This has become less important the older they have grown, but it has yet to become unimportant. Countless other fathers could be available for none of this. Their work - not their choice - kept them at their respective grindstones, often until early evening.

The joy of ministry is that we pastors are largely free to structure our time according to the bent of our own ways of working and the needs of our families. A friend of mine does her hospital calls in the morning, but I prefer to spend the morning hours in study and do my calling in the early afternoon. The point is, there is nothing that dictates which way is the way that should be followed. My friend can take her way; I can take mine. The same rule of thumb applies to other aspects of ministerial work.

As long as the right work is getting done, congregations should not ride their pastors on this issue or question how time is being spent. I have been helped over the years by persons who have affirmed the goodness of my being home when the kids come home from school, and by persons who have acknowledged with gratitude the discipline of being faithful to posted office hours and to the courtesy of returning telephone calls. As a result, the time that is not my own has not felt like an unbearable burden or an intrusion into family life.

As a newly ordained pastor begins to experience these and other joys of ministry, the satisfaction of being a minister will begin to grow inside his or her soul. These early and positive experiences will seal the call to ministry. Most of us think we have a call going into seminary and believe we have one coming out of seminary. We finally know we have one only after God uses the church and our growing experiences in ministry to convince us of the fact of our call. This convincing grows ever so slowly, almost unnoticeably, until the day comes when a new pastor realizes that, though the work of pastoral ministry is difficult and demanding, this is the very work he or she is cut out to do. To reach this point is to know that pastoral ministry, in spite of - and sometimes because of - the very things that make it difficult, is a wonderful and joy-filled life.